The 8-Week Parts Work Journey

A Beginner's Guide to Healing Your Inner Family and Finding Self-Leadership

Fantine Rachel Cunningham

Copyright © 2025 by Fantine Rachel Cunningham. All rights reserved.

First Edition

ISBN (Paperback): 978-1-923604-02-5

ISBN (eBook): 978-1-923604-03-2

This book is for educational and informational purposes only. The content is not intended to be a substitute for professional medical advice, diagnosis, or treatment. Always seek the advice of your physician or other qualified health provider with any questions you may have regarding a medical condition or mental health concern.

The techniques and practices described in this book are based on established therapeutic frameworks but should not replace professional mental health treatment when such treatment is needed.

While Internal Family Systems (IFS) is a recognized therapeutic approach developed by Dr. Richard Schwartz, this book represents the author's interpretation and application of IFS concepts for self-help purposes. This work is not endorsed by, affiliated with, or approved by Dr. Schwartz, the Center for Self Leadership, or any official IFS organization.

All names used in case examples throughout this book are fictitious and created for illustrative purposes only. Any resemblance to actual persons, living or dead, is purely coincidental. The scenarios described are composite examples based on common patterns and do not represent specific individuals.

If you are experiencing suicidal thoughts, severe depression, trauma symptoms, or any mental health crisis, please contact a mental health professional immediately or call a crisis hotline in your area.

The author and publisher disclaim any liability arising directly or indirectly from the use of this book.

Table of Contents

Section I: Welcome to Your Internal Family (Weeks 1-2) 4
- Chapter 1: You Have Parts 1
- Chapter 2: Meeting Your Protectors - The Guards at the Gate 8
- Chapter 3: Understanding Exiles - Your Wounded Inner Children 18
- Chapter 4: Finding Your Self - The Calm, Compassionate Core . 29

Section II: Mapping Your System (Weeks 3-4) 42
- Chapter 5: The Parts Mapping Exercise 43
- Chapter 6: Common Parts Everyone Has 54
- Chapter 7: How Parts Interact and Conflict 67
- Chapter 8: Recognizing Blended States 77

Section III: Dialogue and Healing (Weeks 5-6) 88
- Chapter 9: How to Talk to Your Parts 89
- Chapter 10: Negotiating with Protectors 102
- Chapter 11: Safely Approaching Exiles 114
- Chapter 12: The Unburdening Process 127

Section IV: Integration and Daily Life (Weeks 7-8) 140
- Chapter 13: Parts-Aware Decision Making 141
- Chapter 14: Relationships Through an IFS Lens 153
- Chapter 15: Maintaining Self-Leadership 165
- Chapter 16: Your Ongoing IFS Practice 177

References 192

Section I: Welcome to Your Internal Family (Weeks 1-2)

Chapter 1: You Have Parts

Have you ever noticed how you can be completely different people in different situations? Maybe you're confident and decisive at work, but when you visit your parents, you turn into a defensive teenager. Or perhaps you're patient and understanding with your friends, but snap at your partner over the smallest things.

If this sounds familiar, don't worry. You're not losing your mind, and you're definitely not alone. What you're experiencing is completely normal - you just have different **parts** of yourself that show up in different situations.

Think of it this way: inside each of us lives a whole internal family. Just like any family, these parts have different personalities, different jobs, and sometimes they don't get along. Some parts are protective and want to keep you safe. Others carry old wounds and pain. And somewhere in there is your core Self - the calm, wise, compassionate part of you that can help coordinate this internal family.

This is the foundation of Internal Family Systems (IFS), a groundbreaking approach to understanding how our minds work. Created by Dr. Richard Schwartz in the 1980s, IFS has helped millions of people make sense of their inner world and find peace within themselves (Schwartz, 2001).

Why This Changes Everything

Most of us grow up thinking we should be consistent all the time. We judge ourselves harshly when we act differently in various situations. We wonder why we can't just "get it together" and be the person we want to be all the time.

But here's what IFS teaches us: **you're supposed to have different parts**. It's not a flaw in your design - it's how humans are built. Each part developed for a reason, usually to help you survive or cope with life's challenges.

When you were five years old and your parents fought, maybe a part of you learned to be extra good to keep the peace. When you were bullied at school, perhaps another part developed to be tough and never show weakness. When you experienced heartbreak, a part might have decided that staying guarded was the safest option.

These parts aren't problems to be fixed - they're team members who've been doing their best to help you. The issue isn't that you have parts; it's that sometimes they work against each other or take over when they're not needed.

Meet Sarah's Internal Family

Let me tell you about Sarah, a 32-year-old marketing manager who came to therapy feeling like she was "all over the place." At work, she was known as the go-getter who never missed a deadline. Her colleagues saw her as confident and put-together. But at home, she found herself paralyzed by simple decisions like what to make for dinner.

When Sarah started exploring her parts, she discovered quite a cast of characters living inside her:

The Achiever showed up at work, driving her to excel and maintain her professional reputation. This part had learned early on that success meant safety and approval.

The Perfectionist worked overtime, especially on important projects. This part believed that anything less than perfect would lead to criticism and rejection.

The People-Pleaser emerged in social situations, saying yes to everything and everyone, even when Sarah felt overwhelmed.

The Critic provided a running commentary on everything Sarah did, pointing out potential failures before they happened.

The Little Girl carried memories of feeling overlooked as a child and sometimes got scared when Sarah had to make big decisions.

Once Sarah understood that these weren't character flaws but different parts of her trying to help, everything shifted. She could appreciate what each part was trying to do for her while also setting some boundaries about when each part's help was actually needed.

The Science Behind Parts

You might be wondering if this "parts" idea is just a nice metaphor or if there's real science behind it. The answer is both - it's a useful way to think about yourself, and it's backed by solid research.

Neuroscience shows us that our brains are made up of different networks that can operate somewhat independently (Van der Kolk, 2014). When you're in "work mode," certain neural networks are active. When you're in "parent mode" or "friend mode," different networks take the lead. This is why you can feel like different people in different contexts - because, in a very real sense, different parts of your brain are running the show.

Research on IFS therapy has shown significant improvements in symptoms of depression, anxiety, and trauma when people learn to understand and work with their parts. Studies have found that people who practice IFS report feeling more integrated, less conflicted, and better able to handle life's challenges.

Common Questions About Parts

"Does everyone really have parts?"

Yes, absolutely. Having parts is universal - it's how human consciousness works. Some people are more aware of their different parts than others, but everyone has them. The person who seems completely consistent probably just has parts that work well together, or they might not be paying close attention to their internal shifts.

"Is this the same as multiple personality disorder?"

Not at all. In IFS, parts are normal aspects of a healthy mind. Everyone has them, and they're meant to work together under the leadership of the Self. Multiple personality disorder (now called Dissociative Identity Disorder) is a rare condition where parts become so separated that they don't communicate or share memories. That's completely different from the normal parts we all have.

"What if I can't identify my parts?"

Don't worry if this feels abstract at first. Some people immediately recognize their different parts, while others need time to notice them. As you go through your daily life this week, just start paying attention to when you feel or act differently. Notice if there's a shift in your voice, your posture, or your energy when you switch contexts.

Your Parts Are Already Working

Here's something that might surprise you: your parts are already active and working in your life right now. They're not waiting for you to discover them - they're the reason you can adapt to different situations, handle various responsibilities, and navigate complex relationships.

Think about yesterday. Maybe you woke up and a responsible part got you out of bed and ready for the day. At work, a focused part helped you tackle your to-do list. When a friend called with a problem, a caring part listened and offered support. In the evening, perhaps a playful part wanted to watch a funny movie, while a worried part kept thinking about tomorrow's meeting.

All of this is happening naturally. The goal of IFS isn't to create parts - they're already there. The goal is to become aware of them and help them work together better.

Why Traditional Self-Help Falls Short

Most self-help approaches try to get you to be consistent - to choose one way of being and stick with it. They might tell you to "just be confident" or "stop being so sensitive." But this creates internal conflict because it ignores the reality of your parts.

When a self-help book tells you to "think positive," it's talking to just one part of you while ignoring the part that's genuinely worried or sad. When it says "just say no," it's addressing your boundary-setting part while ignoring the people-pleasing part that developed for good reasons.

IFS takes a different approach. Instead of trying to eliminate certain aspects of yourself, it helps you understand why all your parts developed and how they can work together. This creates lasting change because you're working with your natural psychology, not against it.

The Path Forward

Over the next eight weeks, you're going to become an expert on your own internal family. You'll learn to recognize your different parts, understand what they're trying to do for you, and help them coordinate better. You'll discover your Self - that calm, compassionate core that can provide leadership for your whole system.

This isn't about becoming a different person. It's about becoming more fully yourself - all of your parts working together under wise leadership, rather than competing or taking over at inappropriate times.

Some weeks will feel easier than others. Your parts might resist this process sometimes, especially the ones whose job it is to protect you from change or vulnerability. That's normal and actually a good sign - it means your protective parts are paying attention and doing their job.

Starting to Notice

For this first week, your only job is to start noticing. You don't need to analyze or change anything yet. Just begin to observe when you feel different, when your energy shifts, or when you find yourself acting in ways that surprise you.

Pay attention to:

- How you act differently with different people
- Changes in your internal voice or self-talk
- Shifts in your energy or motivation throughout the day
- Times when you feel conflicted about decisions
- Moments when you surprise yourself with your reactions

Remember, there's no wrong way to have parts. Some people have very distinct parts with clear boundaries. Others experience more subtle shifts and blends. Some parts are loud and obvious, while others are quiet and subtle. All of this is normal.

Your internal family is unique to you, shaped by your experiences, your personality, and your life circumstances. The goal isn't to have the "right" parts - it's to understand and work with the parts you have.

What Makes IFS Different

Unlike other therapy approaches that focus on symptoms or behaviors, IFS looks at the whole internal system. It assumes that every part of you developed for a good reason and deserves to be understood, not eliminated.

This approach tends to create less internal resistance because nothing in you is being pathologized or attacked. Instead, you're developing curiosity and compassion for all aspects of yourself. Research shows that this self-compassionate approach leads to more sustainable change than self-critical approaches (Neff, 2015).

Moving Forward Together

As we continue this journey together, remember that you're not just reading about IFS - you're beginning to experience it. Every time you notice a shift in yourself, every moment of curiosity about your inner world, every instance of treating yourself with a little more compassion - that's IFS in action.

Your parts have been with you your whole life, helping you navigate challenges and opportunities. Now you're going to get to know them better and help them work together more effectively. This is the beginning of a new relationship with yourself - one based on understanding, acceptance, and skilled leadership rather than criticism and control.

What You'll Discover

By the end of these eight weeks, you'll have practical tools for:

- Recognizing when different parts are active
- Understanding what each part needs and wants
- Negotiating between conflicting parts
- Accessing your Self-leadership in challenging situations
- Making decisions that honor all parts of yourself
- Reducing internal conflict and criticism

But more than tools, you'll have a new way of being with yourself. Instead of fighting against aspects of your personality, you'll understand how to work with your whole internal system. Instead of judging yourself for being inconsistent, you'll appreciate the complexity and wisdom of your inner world.

This week, just begin to notice. Your parts are already there, already working, already trying to help you. Now you're going to start getting acquainted with them properly. Welcome to your internal family - they've been waiting to meet you.

Chapter 2: Meeting Your Protectors - The Guards at the Gate

Remember when you were a kid and someone bigger than you threatened to take your lunch money? What did you do? Maybe you learned to avoid that person. Perhaps you got really good at making friends with the tough kids. Or maybe you developed a sharp tongue that could cut down anyone who messed with you.

Whatever strategy you developed, it worked. You kept your lunch money, your dignity, or your safety. And somewhere inside you, a **protector part** was born.

Protectors are the parts of you that learned how to keep you safe, successful, and accepted in the world. They're like security guards for your internal system, always scanning for potential threats and jumping into action when they sense danger.

The thing is, these protector parts never got the memo that you're not in elementary school anymore. They're still using the same strategies that worked when you were seven, fifteen, or twenty-five - even when those strategies don't fit your current situation.

The Protector's Job Description

If protector parts had a job description, it might look something like this:

Wanted: Dedicated individual to prevent bad things from happening. Must be willing to work 24/7 with no breaks. Previous experience in crisis management preferred. Job duties include:

- *Scanning environment for potential threats*
- *Developing strategies to avoid rejection, failure, or harm*

- *Taking control when things get dangerous*
- *Maintaining image and reputation at all costs*
- *Preventing vulnerable parts from getting hurt again*

Your protectors take this job very seriously. They developed their strategies through trial and error, learning what worked in your family, your school, your early relationships. Once they found something that worked, they stuck with it.

The problem is that protectors can be a bit... inflexible. They tend to see the world through the lens of past experiences, applying old solutions to new problems. This is why you might find yourself people-pleasing with your boss the same way you did with a difficult parent, or why you might withdraw from intimacy using the same strategy that protected you from childhood bullying.

Meet the Common Protector Types

While everyone's protector parts are unique, there are some common types that show up frequently. See if you recognize any of these:

The Achiever believes that success equals safety. This part drives you to work harder, accomplish more, and constantly prove your worth. The Achiever learned that being successful brings approval and security, so it keeps pushing you to do better, get promoted, earn more, achieve the next goal.

Marcus, a 28-year-old lawyer, had an Achiever part that had been running his life since high school. This part believed that any rest or relaxation was dangerous because someone else might get ahead. Marcus worked 70-hour weeks, checked email constantly, and felt anxious whenever he wasn't being productive. His Achiever part was trying to protect him from the shame and fear he'd felt as a kid when his parents expressed disappointment in his grades.

The People-Pleaser learned that keeping others happy keeps you safe. This part says yes to everything, avoids conflict, and constantly monitors others' moods to prevent rejection. The People-Pleaser developed in environments where someone's anger or disappointment felt threatening.

The Controller believes that if you can just manage everything perfectly, nothing bad will happen. This part makes detailed plans, tries to anticipate every outcome, and gets anxious when things feel unpredictable. The Controller often develops in chaotic environments where having some control felt like survival.

The Performer learned that being entertaining, impressive, or special brings love and attention. This part works hard to be interesting, funny, or remarkable in some way. The Performer often develops when a child learned that being "regular" meant being invisible or unimportant.

The Rebel protects by rejecting before being rejected. This part might act out, break rules, or push people away before they can leave. The Rebel often formed when conformity felt dangerous or when previous attempts at fitting in led to hurt.

The Caretaker focuses on others' needs to avoid dealing with their own vulnerability. This part becomes indispensable by being helpful, supportive, and always available. The Caretaker learned that being needed felt safer than being needy.

How Protectors Develop

Protectors don't just appear randomly. They develop in response to specific experiences and environments. Understanding how your protectors formed can help you appreciate why they're so committed to their strategies.

Let's say you grew up in a family where emotions were seen as weakness. When you cried, you might have been told to "toughen up" or "stop being so sensitive." Over time, a Tough Guy protector might have developed, learning to stuff down feelings and project strength at all times.

Or maybe you had a parent who was overwhelmed and stressed. You learned that being helpful and easy-going kept the peace and maybe even earned you some positive attention. A Helper protector developed, becoming skilled at reading others' needs and meeting them before being asked.

Perhaps you experienced bullying or rejection at school. A Social Chameleon protector might have formed, learning to adapt to whatever group you were with, changing your personality to fit in and avoid being targeted.

These protectors worked. They helped you navigate difficult situations and kept you safe. The problem is that they often keep working even when the original threat is long gone.

The Protector's Dilemma

Here's the tricky thing about protectors: they're often really good at their jobs. They help you succeed at work, maintain relationships, avoid conflict, and navigate social situations. So why would you want to change them?

The issue isn't that protectors are bad - it's that they can become rigid and take over your entire system. When a protector is "blended" with you (more on this in Chapter 8), it's like that part is driving the bus and you're just along for the ride.

Take Jennifer, a successful marketing executive whose Achiever protector helped her climb the corporate ladder. This part worked incredibly hard, maintained high standards, and delivered excellent results. But when Jennifer got married, her Achiever couldn't figure out how to relax. It kept trying to "achieve" at marriage the same way it achieved at work - setting goals, measuring progress, optimizing performance. Her husband felt like he was married to a life coach instead of a partner.

Jennifer's Achiever wasn't wrong or bad - it just didn't know when to step back and let other parts of her show up in the relationship.

Recognizing Your Protectors

Protectors often feel so natural that you might not recognize them as parts at all. They might feel like "just who you are." But here are some signs that a protector part is active:

Energy shifts: You might notice changes in your posture, voice, or energy when certain protectors take over. The People-Pleaser might make your voice softer and more accommodating. The Tough Guy might make your jaw clench and your shoulders square.

Automatic responses: Protectors often react before you even think about it. If you find yourself saying yes before you've considered whether you want to do something, that might be a People-Pleaser protector. If you immediately start problem-solving when someone shares a feeling, that could be a Fixer protector.

Internal pressure: Protectors often create a sense of urgency or pressure. "I have to get this perfect." "I can't let them see me struggle." "I need to make sure everyone's okay." This pressure comes from the protector's belief that something bad will happen if they don't do their job.

Repetitive patterns: If you find yourself stuck in the same patterns across different relationships or situations, protectors are likely involved. The same conflicts, the same reactions, the same strategies that aren't quite working but you keep trying anyway.

The Protective Continuum

Not all protectors operate the same way. Some are subtle and work behind the scenes, while others are obvious and take charge directly. Understanding this can help you recognize your own protective patterns.

Subtle Protectors might:

- Carefully choose words to avoid conflict
- Dress in ways that send specific messages

- Use humor to deflect serious conversations
- Stay busy to avoid difficult feelings
- Maintain a particular image on social media

Obvious Protectors might:

- Take charge in group situations
- Argue when they feel criticized
- Work late to ensure everything is perfect
- Give advice even when not asked
- Avoid situations that feel risky or vulnerable

Both types are doing important work, but they require different approaches when you want to work with them.

When Protectors Conflict

Sometimes your protectors disagree with each other about the best strategy, creating internal conflict. This is incredibly common and can feel very confusing.

David had a People-Pleaser protector that wanted him to say yes to every social invitation to maintain his friendships. But he also had an Achiever protector that believed he needed to work evenings and weekends to get ahead in his career. These two parts were constantly in conflict, leaving David feeling guilty no matter what he chose.

Sarah had a Controller protector that wanted to plan every detail of her vacation to ensure it went smoothly. But she also had a Spontaneous protector that believed rigid planning would ruin the fun and make her seem uptight to her friends. The internal argument between these parts left her feeling paralyzed and unable to make any plans at all.

When protectors conflict, it's usually because they're trying to protect you from different threats. The People-Pleaser fears rejection, while the Achiever fears failure. The Controller fears chaos, while the Spontaneous part fears being seen as boring or rigid.

Working With Your Protectors

The goal isn't to get rid of your protectors - that would be impossible and unwise. These parts developed to help you, and they often continue to serve important functions in your life. The goal is to develop a better working relationship with them.

This means:

Appreciation: Understanding what each protector is trying to do for you and thanking them for their efforts, even when their strategies aren't working perfectly.

Negotiation: Learning to talk with your protectors about when their help is needed and when other parts might handle a situation better.

Leadership: Developing your Self-leadership so that you can coordinate your protectors rather than being taken over by them.

Updates: Helping protectors learn about your current life situation so they can adjust their strategies accordingly.

The Protector's Fear

Understanding what your protectors are afraid of is key to working with them effectively. Every protective strategy is designed to prevent something specific from happening. Until you understand what that something is, your protector will keep using the same old strategies.

The Achiever might be afraid of being seen as lazy or worthless. The People-Pleaser might fear abandonment or anger. The Controller might be terrified of chaos or unpredictability. The Performer might fear being boring or invisible.

These fears usually trace back to early experiences where these things actually happened or felt like real threats. Your five-year-old self learned that dad got really angry when things were messy, so a Controller part developed to keep everything organized. Your teenage self learned that being funny got you accepted by the popular kids, so a Performer part learned to entertain.

The fears were real then, and your protectors' solutions worked. The question for your adult self is whether these strategies are still necessary and helpful in your current life.

Protectors and Relationships

Protectors have a huge impact on your relationships, often in ways you might not realize. They determine how you show up with others, what you're willing to share, how you handle conflict, and what you need from your connections.

Sometimes protectors help relationships by making you more considerate, responsible, or engaging. But they can also create distance when they're working too hard to maintain a certain image or avoid certain risks.

Lisa's Perfectionist protector helped her be a reliable friend who always showed up prepared and put-together. But it also prevented her from being vulnerable or asking for help, which made her friends feel like they couldn't really get close to her.

Mike's Funny Guy protector made him popular at parties and helped him deflect conflict with humor. But when his girlfriend wanted to have serious conversations about their relationship, his protector kept making jokes, leaving her feeling like he didn't care about her concerns.

Signs Your Protectors Need Support

How do you know when your protectors are working too hard or using outdated strategies? Here are some signs:

Exhaustion: If you're constantly tired even when you're not physically active, a protector might be working overtime.

Rigidity: When you can't imagine acting differently even in situations where your current approach isn't working.

Internal criticism: Harsh self-talk often comes from protectors who are afraid you'll make mistakes.

Relationship patterns: Repeating the same dynamics across multiple relationships usually indicates protector strategies at work.

Physical symptoms: Tension, headaches, digestive issues, and other stress-related symptoms can signal that protectors are on high alert.

Decision paralysis: Sometimes protectors disagree so strongly that you can't choose any course of action.

Your Protectors This Week

For this week, your job is simply to start noticing your protectors. You don't need to change them or even fully understand them yet. Just begin to recognize when they're active.

Pay attention to:

- When you feel like you "should" do something
- Times when you automatically respond without thinking
- Situations where you feel pressure or urgency
- Moments when you're trying to manage others' reactions
- Internal conversations about what's safe or dangerous

Remember, your protectors are on your team. They might be using outdated strategies, but their intention is always to help you. As you start to notice them this week, try approaching them with curiosity rather than criticism.

You might even try thanking them. "Thanks, People-Pleaser, for trying to keep me liked." "Thanks, Achiever, for helping me stay motivated." This might feel strange at first, but appreciation is the foundation of good relationships - including relationships with your own parts.

Moving Forward

Next week, we'll explore another type of part - your exiles. These are the parts that carry your deepest wounds and most authentic feelings. Your protectors work so hard partly because they're trying to keep these exile parts safe and hidden.

But for now, just focus on getting to know your protectors. They've been working hard for you, probably for many years. It's time to acknowledge their efforts and start building a more conscious partnership with them.

Your protectors aren't obstacles to overcome - they're resources to understand and coordinate. When you learn to work with them skillfully, they become powerful allies in creating the life you actually want.

Chapter 3: Understanding Exiles - Your Wounded Inner Children

Picture a house where all the adults are working frantically to keep everything looking perfect from the outside. They're painting the shutters, mowing the lawn, answering the door with big smiles, and making sure no one sees anything messy or broken. Meanwhile, locked away in the basement, there's a child who's been crying for hours because they're hurt, scared, and alone.

This is what happens in your internal system when your exile parts get pushed away and hidden. Your protectors (the adults in this metaphor) work overtime to keep these wounded parts locked away because they believe that if anyone saw the hurt, scared, young parts of you, something terrible would happen.

Exiles are the parts of you that carry your deepest wounds, your most authentic feelings, and often your greatest creativity and joy. They're called exiles because they've been banished from everyday life, pushed into the background by protectors who believe they're too dangerous, needy, or vulnerable to be allowed out.

But here's the thing about that crying child in the basement: they're not going away just because they're locked up. In fact, they're probably getting louder, more desperate, and more creative about getting attention. And until someone goes down to that basement with compassion and care, the adults upstairs will have to keep working harder and harder to maintain the illusion that everything's fine.

What Exile Parts Carry

Exile parts typically carry the experiences and feelings that were too overwhelming, painful, or unacceptable when they happened. These might include:

Young feelings: The pure joy, wonder, creativity, and spontaneity that you had as a child before life taught you to be careful, practical, or "appropriate."

Wounds and pain: Experiences of rejection, abandonment, abuse, criticism, or neglect that were too much for your young system to handle at the time.

Unmet needs: The longing for love, attention, acceptance, safety, or understanding that wasn't adequately met during important developmental periods.

Authentic self: The real you - your genuine preferences, desires, dreams, and ways of being before you learned to adapt and protect yourself.

Difficult emotions: Sadness, fear, anger, shame, or loneliness that your family or environment couldn't handle, so these feelings got pushed underground.

How Exiles Get Created

Exiles don't start out as exiles. They begin as natural, spontaneous parts of childhood - the parts that laugh easily, cry when hurt, get excited about small things, and love openly without reservation.

These parts become exiles when the environment can't handle their full expression. This doesn't necessarily mean there was abuse or trauma (though that certainly creates exiles). Sometimes exile parts form in families that are just overwhelmed, emotionally unavailable, or have rigid rules about which feelings are acceptable.

Let me tell you about Maria's story. When Maria was six, her parents went through a bitter divorce. Her mother, overwhelmed with her own pain, couldn't handle Maria's confusion and sadness about the family breaking apart. When Maria cried or asked questions, her mother would say things like, "Don't be such a baby," or "You need to be strong for Mommy."

Maria's natural childhood part - the one that needed comfort, reassurance, and space to feel sad about this big change - had to go into exile. A protector part developed that learned to be "strong," never complain, and take care of other people's feelings instead of her own.

Thirty years later, Maria still struggled to acknowledge her own needs or ask for support. Her exile part was still locked away, still carrying that six-year-old's sadness and confusion, while her protector parts worked frantically to make sure she never appeared needy or weak.

The Exile's Persistence

Here's something important to understand about exile parts: **they don't age**. While your protectors mature and develop sophisticated strategies, your exiles remain frozen at the age they were when they went underground.

This is why you might have reactions that seem completely out of proportion to the current situation. When your boss criticizes your work, you might feel that crushing shame and terror that belongs to your eight-year-old exile who was humiliated in front of the class. When your partner seems distant, you might experience the desperate panic of your five-year-old exile who thought Daddy left because they were bad.

The exile isn't overreacting to your current situation - they're reacting to the original situation they never got to finish processing.

Common Exile Experiences

While everyone's exile parts are unique, there are some common themes in how they were created and what they carry:

The Sensitive Child who was told they were "too much" - too emotional, too intense, too needy. This exile learned that their natural sensitivity was a problem and went into hiding to avoid being criticized or rejected.

The Creative Dreamer who was told to "be realistic" or "stop living in a fantasy world." This exile carries your imagination, artistic impulses, and biggest dreams, but learned these weren't valued or safe to express.

The Angry Kid who was told that anger was bad, scary, or unacceptable. This exile carries your natural response to injustice, boundary violations, and mistreatment, but learned that expressing anger brought punishment or abandonment.

The Joyful Spirit who learned that being too happy, excited, or exuberant was annoying or inappropriate. This exile carries your natural enthusiasm and zest for life but was taught to tone it down.

The Scared Child who experienced something frightening and overwhelming without adequate support. This exile carries trauma, terror, and the need for safety and protection.

The Rejected Kid who experienced significant abandonment, neglect, or rejection. This exile carries the pain of not being wanted and the deep longing to be loved and accepted.

Why Protectors Exile These Parts

Your protector parts don't exile these vulnerable aspects of you out of cruelty - they do it out of love and fear. From the protectors' perspective, these exile parts are dangerous because:

They might get hurt again: If you let your trusting, loving part out, they might get rejected or betrayed again. If you show your creative, dreamy side, people might criticize or dismiss you again.

They might make you look weak: Protectors often believe that vulnerability equals weakness, and weakness brings danger. Better to keep those needy, emotional parts hidden than risk being seen as incapable or damaged.

They might overwhelm others: If your exile parts carry big emotions or needs, protectors worry that expressing these will drive people away or create chaos.

They might take over: Sometimes exile parts, when they do break free, can flood the system with intense emotions or young ways of thinking. Protectors work hard to prevent this kind of "emotional hijacking."

The problem is that exiling these parts doesn't make them disappear - it just makes them more desperate and reactive when they do surface.

How Exiles Influence Your Life

Even when they're locked away, exile parts have a huge impact on your daily life. They influence your choices, relationships, triggers, and the overall quality of your emotional experience.

Relationship patterns: Your exile parts often determine what you're looking for in relationships. If you have an exile that carries abandonment wounds, you might find yourself either clinging desperately to partners or pushing them away before they can leave you.

Career choices: Sometimes people choose careers that allow their exiles to heal vicariously. Someone with an exiled Creative Dreamer might become a teacher to nurture other people's creativity, or someone with a Rejected Kid exile might go into helping professions to ensure others don't feel unwanted.

Triggers and reactions: When something in your current life resembles the original situation that created an exile, that part can get activated and flood you with old emotions. This is why you might have surprisingly strong reactions to situations that don't seem that significant to others.

Self-sabotage: Sometimes exile parts create problems as a way of getting attention. If the only way your Scared Child exile ever got care was when you were sick or in crisis, that part might unconsciously create crises to get the attention it needs.

Physical symptoms: Exile parts often express themselves through the body when they can't be expressed emotionally. Chronic pain, digestive issues, fatigue, and other physical symptoms sometimes carry the emotional pain of exile parts.

The Exile's Gifts

While exile parts carry pain and wounds, they also carry some of your most precious qualities. When exile parts feel safe enough to come out of hiding, they often bring:

Creativity and imagination: Many of your most creative impulses come from exile parts that haven't been trained out of thinking outside the box.

Authentic emotion: Exiles carry your genuine feelings - both painful and joyful - without the filters that protectors apply.

Spontaneity and playfulness: The ability to be present, silly, and spontaneous often lives in exile parts that remember how to be childlike (not childish).

Intuition and wisdom: Young parts often have access to intuitive knowing that gets educated out of us as we learn to rely solely on rational thinking.

Capacity for wonder: The ability to be amazed, delighted, and fascinated by life often lives in exile parts that haven't become jaded or cynical.

Deep love and connection: Your capacity for intimate, authentic connection often comes from exile parts that haven't learned to protect themselves from vulnerability.

Jake's Story: When Exiles Break Free

Jake was a 35-year-old accountant who prided himself on being rational, reliable, and even-tempered. His protector parts had created a stable life - good job, nice house, long-term relationship. But Jake felt increasingly empty and disconnected, like he was living someone else's life.

During a particularly stressful period at work, Jake's girlfriend suggested they take a weekend trip to the mountains. On the second day, they were hiking when Jake saw a waterfall that reminded him of a place his grandfather used to take him as a child.

Suddenly, Jake was sobbing. Not just crying, but deep, body-shaking sobs that seemed to come from nowhere. His girlfriend was alarmed, but Jake couldn't explain what was happening. He just felt overwhelmed by grief and longing.

What Jake was experiencing was an exile part breaking through - the part of him that had loved those adventures with his grandfather, who had felt safe to be curious and excited about nature. This part had gone into exile when Jake's parents divorced when he was ten and he had to become "the responsible one" who didn't cause problems or have needs.

The waterfall had awakened this exiled part, and thirty years of unexpressed grief and longing came flooding out. Once Jake understood what was happening, he was able to give this part the attention and care it had been seeking. The result was that Jake felt more alive and connected than he had in decades.

Recognizing Your Exiles

Exile parts often stay hidden, so recognizing them can be more challenging than noticing protectors. Here are some signs that exile parts are trying to get your attention:

Disproportionate reactions: When your emotional response seems much bigger than the situation warrants, an exile part may be activated.

Sudden mood changes: If you go from feeling fine to feeling devastated, furious, or terrified without a clear reason, an exile might have been triggered.

Body sensations: Exiles often communicate through physical sensations - tightness in your chest, knots in your stomach, tension in your shoulders.

Dreams and fantasies: Exile parts sometimes express themselves through dreams, daydreams, or creative fantasies.

Addictive behaviors: Sometimes exile parts try to get their needs met through substances, shopping, food, or other compulsive behaviors.

Chronic dissatisfaction: A persistent sense that something is missing from your life, even when things look good on paper, often signals exiles that aren't being acknowledged.

The Exile's Dilemma

Exile parts are caught in a terrible bind. They carry authentic needs and feelings that are essential to your wholeness, but they've learned that expressing these parts of themselves brings rejection, criticism, or abandonment.

So they develop desperate strategies to get attention:

- They might create drama or crisis
- They might sabotage good things in your life
- They might express themselves through physical symptoms
- They might attach to people who treat them the way they were originally treated
- They might flood you with overwhelming emotions at inappropriate times

None of these strategies work very well, but exile parts don't know what else to do. They're stuck using the tools they had available when they were young.

What Exiles Need

What exile parts need most is what they needed originally but didn't get: **witnessing, validation, and care**. They need someone (ideally your Self) to:

See them: To acknowledge their existence, their pain, and their legitimate needs without trying to fix, change, or minimize their experience.

Believe them: To trust their perspective on what happened and validate that their reactions made sense given their experience.

Care for them: To offer comfort, protection, and nurturing - not to make the pain go away, but to provide companionship in the midst of it.

Give them what they needed: Sometimes this is symbolic - imagining giving your scared child the safety they needed, or your creative child the encouragement they craved.

Include them: To find appropriate ways for these parts to be present in your current life rather than keeping them locked away.

The Path to Healing

Healing exile parts isn't about re-experiencing trauma or drowning in old pain. It's about developing a relationship with these parts from your current, adult Self - the part of you that has resources, wisdom, and the capacity to provide what these young parts need.

This process typically involves:

Recognition: Becoming aware that these parts exist and understanding how they were created.

Relationship: Developing a caring connection with these parts instead of avoiding or minimizing them.

Retrieval: Helping these parts know that they don't have to stay stuck in the past - that they can come into your current life where they'll be protected and valued.

Integration: Finding healthy ways for these parts to express themselves and contribute to your life.

Your Exiles This Week

This week, your task is to begin noticing when exile parts might be present. This requires a gentle touch - exile parts often hide when they sense too much attention too quickly.

Pay attention to:

- Moments when your emotions feel surprisingly intense
- Times when you feel much younger than your chronological age
- Physical sensations that don't seem connected to current circumstances
- Memories or images from childhood that pop up unexpectedly
- Feelings of emptiness or longing that you can't quite explain

If you notice what might be an exile part, try approaching it with curiosity and gentleness rather than judgment or alarm. You might even try sending some appreciation: "Thank you for trying to get my attention. I want to understand what you need."

Remember, exile parts have often been hurt by being ignored, criticized, or pushed away. They need to know that this time will be different - that you're approaching them as an ally, not another person who will reject them.

Moving Forward

Next week, we'll explore your Self - the part of you that has the capacity to provide leadership, compassion, and healing for both your protectors and your exiles. Your Self is what makes it possible to work with all your parts from a place of wisdom rather than being taken over by them.

But for now, just begin to acknowledge that you have parts that carry wounds and authentic feelings. These parts aren't problems to be solved - they're aspects of yourself that need to be understood and cared for.

Your exile parts have been waiting patiently (or not so patiently) for you to turn toward them with compassion. They carry not only your wounds but also your deepest capacity for joy, creativity, and authentic connection.

The journey toward these parts requires courage, but it's one of the most important trips you'll ever take. These parts of you have been in exile long enough. It's time to bring them home.

Chapter 4: Finding Your Self - The Calm, Compassionate Core

Imagine you're at a family reunion where everyone's arguing. Your uncle is complaining loudly about politics, your cousin is trying to keep the peace by changing the subject every two minutes, your teenage nephew is sulking in the corner, and your aunt is frantically running around trying to make sure everyone has enough food.

Now imagine that in the middle of all this chaos, there's one person who remains calm. They're not trying to control anyone or fix anything. They're just present - listening when someone needs to be heard, offering gentle suggestions when asked, and somehow creating a sense of stability just by being there.

That person at the family reunion? That's what your **Self** is like in your internal family system.

Your Self isn't another part - it's the core of who you are underneath all your protective strategies and wounded reactions. It's the part of you that can witness your parts without being taken over by them, care for them without becoming them, and provide the kind of leadership that allows your whole system to work together.

You might be thinking, "That sounds nice, but I don't feel like I have that calm, wise part. Most of the time I feel like I'm being run by my anxious thoughts or my people-pleasing tendencies or my inner critic."

Here's the thing: **everyone has Self**. It might be buried under years of protective strategies, or it might only show up in certain situations, but it's there. In fact, you've probably experienced your Self more often than you realize.

Recognizing Self-Leadership

Self-energy has some distinctive qualities that you can learn to recognize. When you're in Self-leadership (as opposed to being blended with or taken over by parts), you tend to feel:

Curious rather than judgmental. Instead of immediately deciding that something is good or bad, right or wrong, you find yourself wanting to understand what's really going on.

Compassionate toward yourself and others. You can see struggling or difficult behavior as a sign that someone (including you) is hurting rather than being bad or wrong.

Calm even in stressful situations. This doesn't mean you're emotionless, but rather that you're not hijacked by intense emotions. You can feel your feelings without being overwhelmed by them.

Connected to your values and to others. You have a clear sense of what matters to you, and you can maintain genuine connection even during conflict or difficulty.

Creative in your problem-solving. Instead of falling back on the same old strategies, you can find new approaches and see possibilities that weren't obvious before.

Clear about boundaries and priorities. You know what's yours to handle and what isn't, what you can control and what you can't.

Courageous in the face of uncertainty. You can move forward even when you don't know exactly how things will turn out.

When You've Experienced Self

Think back through your life to moments when you felt most like yourself - not performing or protecting or reacting, just being authentically you. These were probably moments of Self-leadership.

Maybe it was:

- A time when you were in nature and felt completely peaceful and present
- A moment when someone was upset and you were able to listen without trying to fix them
- A situation where you stood up for something important without being aggressive or defensive
- A creative project where you lost track of time and felt completely engaged
- A conversation where you shared something vulnerable and felt genuinely connected
- A crisis where you found yourself naturally stepping up to help and coordinate

Sarah remembered being eight years old, playing in her backyard after a rainstorm. She was fascinated by the way water moved in tiny rivers down the hillside, and she spent hours building little dams and bridges with sticks and stones. She felt completely absorbed, peaceful, and alive. Looking back, she realized this was one of the clearest experiences of her Self she could remember - curious, creative, present, and completely free from the anxious, people-pleasing parts that usually dominated her experience.

Marcus recalled a time when his best friend's father died suddenly. While everyone else was either falling apart or trying to cheer his friend up, Marcus found himself just sitting with his friend, not saying much, but somehow providing exactly the kind of steady, caring presence his friend needed. He wasn't trying to be helpful - he just naturally was.

Self vs. Parts

One of the most important distinctions in IFS is the difference between Self and parts. Parts have jobs to do, strategies to employ, and particular ways of seeing the world. Self has no agenda other than understanding, caring, and responding wisely to whatever is happening.

Parts are:
- Focused on specific concerns or strategies
- Often reactive to triggers from the past
- Trying to prevent certain outcomes or achieve certain goals
- Limited in their perspective
- Sometimes in conflict with other parts

Self is:
- Naturally wise and spacious
- Responsive to current reality rather than past triggers
- Curious about all perspectives without being attached to particular outcomes
- Able to see the bigger picture
- Naturally able to coordinate and harmonize different parts

This doesn't mean Self is better than parts - just that Self and parts have different functions. Parts are like skilled specialists; Self is like a good manager who can help coordinate the specialists effectively.

The Self-Obscuring Parts

If Self is natural and everyone has it, why doesn't it feel accessible most of the time? The answer is that certain parts specialize in taking over and blending with your sense of identity. These are sometimes called "Self-obscuring parts" because they make it hard to access your natural Self-leadership.

The Critic convinces you that harsh self-judgment is necessary for improvement. When this part is blended, you think you ARE someone who needs constant correction rather than someone who HAS a part that learned to use criticism as a motivational strategy.

The Anxious Mind floods your system with worried thoughts and catastrophic predictions. When blended with this part, you believe you ARE an anxious person rather than someone who HAS a part that tries to prevent bad outcomes by thinking through every possibility.

The People-Pleaser takes over your decision-making to keep others happy. When this part is blended, you think you ARE someone who just naturally cares more about others than yourself, rather than someone who HAS a part that learned people-pleasing as a survival strategy.

The Controller tries to manage outcomes by controlling circumstances and people. When blended, you think you ARE someone who needs to be in charge rather than someone who HAS a part that learned control as a way to feel safe.

Accessing Self-Leadership

The good news is that accessing Self isn't about creating something new - it's about uncovering what's already there. Self-leadership becomes available when parts trust enough to step back and let Self take the lead.

This happens through a process of:

Noticing when you're blended: Learning to recognize when a part has taken over your perspective rather than informing it.

Creating space: Using techniques like deep breathing, mindfulness, or simply pausing to create some distance between you and the part that's activated.

Asking parts to step back: Gently requesting that the activated part give you some space to think clearly.

Connecting with Self-qualities: Intentionally cultivating curiosity, compassion, and calmness.

Listening to parts from Self: Once you have some access to Self-energy, using that spaciousness to understand what your parts are trying to tell you.

The Self-Leadership Process

Here's a practical example of how this works:

Imagine you've just been criticized by your boss, and you're feeling a familiar flood of shame and self-attack. Instead of being swept away by these feelings, you might:

1. **Notice**: "Wow, I'm really activated right now. This feels like that part of me that gets overwhelmed by criticism."

2. **Pause**: Take a few deep breaths and create some internal space.

3. **Ask for space**: "Hey, Shame part, I can see you're really upset. Can you give me a little room so I can think clearly about this situation?"

4. **Connect with Self**: Feel your feet on the ground, your breath moving in and out, and access that calmer, more spacious part of yourself.

5. **Listen from Self**: "Okay, Shame part, tell me what you're worried about. What are you trying to protect me from?"

6. **Respond wisely**: From this Self-led place, you might realize that the criticism was actually helpful feedback, or that your boss was having a bad day, or that you want to have a conversation about the situation. Whatever response emerges will be more skillful than reacting from the blended shame.

Self-Leadership in Relationships

One of the most powerful applications of Self-leadership is in your relationships with others. When you're in Self, you can:

Stay present during conflict instead of getting hijacked by defensive parts or parts that want to attack back.

Listen to understand rather than listening to defend or prepare your rebuttal.

Respond to what's actually happening rather than reacting to past hurts or future fears.

Maintain your own boundaries while still caring about the other person's experience.

Stay connected to your values even when someone is trying to manipulate or pressure you.

Jennifer discovered this during a difficult conversation with her mother. Usually, these conversations would activate Jennifer's Rebellious Teenager part, which would get defensive and sarcastic, leading to hurt feelings on both sides.

This time, Jennifer noticed when her Rebellious part got activated and asked it to step back. From Self, she could see that her mother's criticism was coming from her own anxiety about Jennifer's life choices. Instead of defending or attacking, Jennifer was able to say, "Mom, it sounds like you're worried about me. Tell me more about what you're concerned about."

This simple shift - from reaction to curiosity - completely changed the dynamic of their relationship.

Obstacles to Self-Leadership

Several things can make it challenging to access Self-leadership:

Trauma: When someone has experienced significant trauma, protective parts might be so vigilant that they're afraid to let Self lead. In these cases, parts need extra reassurance that Self can actually keep them safe.

Family systems: If you grew up in a family where Self-leadership wasn't modeled or supported, you might not have a clear reference point for what it looks like.

Cultural conditioning: Some cultures emphasize conformity, hierarchy, or emotional suppression in ways that make it difficult to access the authenticity and emotional attunement that characterize Self-leadership.

Current stress: When you're overwhelmed by current circumstances, parts might take over more frequently because they believe the situation requires their particular expertise.

Lack of practice: Like any skill, Self-leadership gets stronger with practice. If you've spent years being run by parts, it takes time to develop the neural pathways for Self-leadership.

Self-Compassion vs. Self-Criticism

One of the clearest signs of Self-leadership is how you relate to your own mistakes and struggles. Parts-driven responses tend toward either harsh self-criticism or defensive justification. Self-led responses are characterized by self-compassion.

Self-criticism (usually from a Critic part) sounds like:

- "I can't believe I did that again. I'm such an idiot."
- "Everyone else can handle this. What's wrong with me?"
- "I should be better at this by now."

Self-compassion (from Self) sounds like:

- "That didn't go the way I hoped. What can I learn from this?"
- "This is really hard. It makes sense that I'm struggling."
- "I'm human, and humans make mistakes. How can I do better next time?"

Research shows that self-compassion is much more effective than self-criticism for creating positive change (Neff, 2015). Self-criticism activates shame and defensive parts, making it harder to learn and grow. Self-compassion creates the safety necessary for honest self-reflection and genuine improvement.

Developing Your Self-Leadership

Self-leadership isn't something you either have or don't have - it's something you can cultivate and strengthen over time. Here are some ways to develop your capacity for Self-leadership:

Mindfulness practices: Regular meditation, breathing exercises, or other mindfulness practices help you create space between you and your parts.

Body awareness: Paying attention to physical sensations helps you notice when parts are activated and gives you a pathway back to Self.

Journaling: Writing can help you sort out which voices in your head are parts and which insights are coming from Self.

Time in nature: Many people find it easier to access Self-energy when they're in natural settings.

Creative activities: Art, music, writing, or other creative pursuits often provide access to Self-energy.

Therapy or coaching: Working with someone skilled in parts work can help you identify and work with the specific parts that most interfere with your Self-leadership.

Self-Leadership and Decision Making

One of the most practical applications of Self-leadership is in making decisions. When parts are driving your choices, decisions often come from fear, people-pleasing, perfectionism, or other part-driven strategies. When Self is leading, decisions come from a place of clarity, values, and wisdom.

Parts-driven decisions might be:

- Taking a job because it pays well (Achiever part) even though it violates your values
- Saying yes to commitments because you don't want to disappoint people (People-Pleaser part) even though you're already overwhelmed
- Avoiding opportunities because they feel risky (Protector part) even though they align with your dreams

Self-led decisions consider:

- What aligns with your deepest values and priorities
- What serves your whole life, not just one aspect of it
- What feels authentic and sustainable over time
- What takes into account both your needs and the impact on others

Your Self This Week

This week, your primary task is to start noticing when you're in Self-leadership versus when you're being driven by parts. This isn't about judgment - both Self and parts have important roles to play. It's about developing awareness so you can choose more consciously who's running the show at any given moment.

Pay attention to:

- Moments when you feel calm and clear, even in stressful situations
- Times when you respond to conflict with curiosity rather than defensiveness
- Situations where you naturally know what to do without overthinking
- Interactions where you feel genuinely connected to others

- Decisions that come from a place of clarity rather than anxiety or pressure

You might also experiment with:

- Taking three deep breaths before responding to stressful situations
- Asking yourself, "What would be most helpful here?" instead of reacting automatically
- Noticing physical sensations as a way of creating space between you and activated parts
- Spending a few minutes each day in quiet reflection or meditation

Over the next four weeks, you'll be learning practical skills for working with your parts from Self-leadership. You'll discover how to map your internal system, dialogue with your parts, and integrate everything you're learning into your daily life.

But all of these skills rest on the foundation of Self-leadership. The more you can access your natural wisdom, compassion, and clarity, the more effective you'll be at creating internal harmony and external change.

Your Self has been there all along, waiting patiently underneath all the protective strategies and wounded reactions. It doesn't need to be created or fixed - just uncovered and trusted.

You already have everything you need to lead your internal family skillfully. The next phase of this journey is about learning to use these natural capacities more consistently and effectively.

Your parts have been working hard to take care of you, often for many years. Now it's time for your Self to take the lead and provide the kind of leadership that allows all parts of you to relax into their best contributions.

Welcome to Self-leadership. This is where the real transformation begins.

What You've Discovered

Congratulations! You've completed the first phase of your IFS journey. Over these past two weeks, you've been introduced to a completely new way of understanding yourself - not as a single, consistent personality, but as an internal family with different parts, each with their own history, strategies, and contributions.

You've met your **protectors** - those dedicated parts that work tirelessly to keep you safe, successful, and accepted. You've begun to recognize how these parts developed and why they use the strategies they do.

You've started to understand your **exiles** - the wounded, authentic parts that carry your deepest pain and your greatest capacity for joy, creativity, and connection. You've learned that these parts don't disappear just because they're pushed away, and that they hold keys to your wholeness.

Most importantly, you've begun to connect with your **Self** - that calm, compassionate core that has the capacity to provide leadership for your entire internal system. You've discovered that this isn't something you need to develop from scratch, but rather something that's already there, waiting to be uncovered and trusted.

As you move into the next phase of this work - mapping your system and learning to dialogue with your parts - remember that this is a practice, not a performance. Some days you'll feel clear and connected to your Self-leadership. Other days, parts will take over and you'll feel like you're back where you started.

This is completely normal. Your parts have been running the show for a long time, and they're not going to step back overnight. Be patient with yourself as you develop these new skills. Your internal family is worth the effort, and you're already making important changes just by bringing awareness to these dynamics.

Next week, you'll start creating a detailed map of your internal system. This is where the work gets both more specific and more practical. You'll learn to identify your unique constellation of parts and understand how they interact with each other.

For now, just appreciate how much you've already learned about yourself. You're not crazy for feeling like different people in different situations. You have parts, and that's exactly how you're supposed to be built. The journey toward integration and self-leadership has begun.

Section II: Mapping Your System (Weeks 3-4)

Chapter 5: The Parts Mapping Exercise

You know that feeling when you're trying to clean out a cluttered garage, but you don't know what's actually in there? You keep bumping into things in the dark, tripping over boxes you forgot existed, and getting frustrated because you can't find what you need when you need it.

That's what it's like trying to navigate your internal world without a clear map of your parts. You know there are different aspects of yourself that show up at different times, but without understanding who they are, what they do, or how they relate to each other, you're basically stumbling around in the dark.

Creating a **parts map** is like turning on the lights in that garage. Suddenly you can see what you're working with, understand how everything fits together, and start organizing things in a way that actually works.

A parts map isn't just an intellectual exercise - it's a practical tool that helps you recognize which part is active at any moment, understand why certain situations trigger particular reactions, and learn how to work with your parts more skillfully.

What Is Parts Mapping

Parts mapping is a structured way of identifying and understanding the different parts that make up your internal system. Think of it as creating a family tree for your psyche - documenting who's who, what their roles are, how they developed, and how they interact with each other.

Unlike traditional therapy approaches that might focus on symptoms or behaviors, parts mapping helps you understand the underlying system that creates those symptoms and behaviors. Instead of just trying to stop being anxious, for example, you learn about the Worried part that creates anxiety, what it's trying to protect you from, and what it needs to feel safe enough to relax.

Research in neuroscience supports the idea that our minds naturally organize into different self-states or network configurations (Siegel, 2012). Parts mapping simply gives you a framework for understanding and working with this natural organization more consciously.

The Benefits of Mapping

When you create a detailed map of your parts, several things happen:

You stop taking everything personally. Instead of thinking "I'm so messed up" when you have a strong reaction, you can think "Oh, that's my Scared Kid part getting triggered by rejection."

You develop compassion for yourself. When you understand how and why your parts developed, it's harder to judge them harshly. You start seeing them as understandable responses to life circumstances rather than character flaws.

You can predict and prepare. Once you know which situations tend to activate which parts, you can prepare for challenging circumstances and have strategies ready.

You reduce internal conflict. When parts feel seen and understood, they're less likely to fight each other for control or attention.

You increase your choices. Instead of being swept away by automatic reactions, you can recognize what's happening and choose how to respond.

Getting Started with Your Map

The first step in creating your parts map is simply paying attention to when you feel different. This might seem obvious, but most of us are so used to our internal shifts that we don't notice them consciously.

Start by tracking moments of transition throughout your day:

- How do you feel when you first wake up versus when you're getting ready for work?
- What happens inside you when you walk into a social gathering versus when you're alone?
- How do you shift when you're talking to your boss versus talking to your best friend?
- What changes when you're faced with a deadline versus when you have free time?

These transitions are usually moments when different parts are taking the lead. Your Responsible part might take over when you're getting ready for work, while your Social part emerges at gatherings and your Anxious part activates under pressure.

The Basic Mapping Process

Here's a step-by-step approach to creating your initial parts map:

Step 1: Notice and Name Start by simply noticing when you feel different and giving those states names. Don't worry about being precise or therapeutic - use whatever names feel natural. You might have:

- Your Work Self
- Your Social Butterfly
- Your Worried Mind
- Your Inner Critic
- Your Fun-Loving Kid
- Your Responsible Adult

Step 2: Get Curious About Each Part For each part you identify, ask yourself:

- When does this part usually show up?

- What does this part care about most?
- What is this part trying to protect me from or help me achieve?
- How old does this part feel?
- What does this part need to feel safe and valued?

Step 3: Understand the Part's History Try to trace each part back to its origins:

- When did you first need this part's particular skills or strategies?
- What was happening in your life when this part developed?
- How did this part help you cope with difficult situations?
- What would have happened if this part hadn't developed?

Step 4: Identify Relationships Between Parts Notice how your parts relate to each other:

- Which parts work well together?
- Which parts tend to conflict?
- Which parts try to shut down or control other parts?
- Which parts are friends versus which ones barely tolerate each other?

Tools for Mapping

Different people respond to different mapping techniques. Here are several approaches you can try:

Visual Mapping Some people find it helpful to create actual visual maps of their parts. You might draw:

- A family tree with different parts as family members
- A house with different parts living in different rooms

- A workplace with different parts having different jobs
- A cast of characters for the movie of your life

Written Profiles Others prefer to write detailed descriptions of each part, like character profiles in a novel. For each part, you might include:

- Name and age
- Physical description (how they look in your imagination)
- Personality traits
- Main concerns and fears
- Preferred strategies
- Relationship to other parts

Body Mapping Many parts express themselves through physical sensations, so mapping where you feel different parts in your body can be useful:

- Where do you feel your Anxious part? (Maybe tension in your chest or butterflies in your stomach)
- Where does your Confident part live? (Perhaps a straightening of your spine or opening of your chest)
- What does your Sad part feel like physically? (Maybe heaviness in your heart or tears behind your eyes)

Lisa's Mapping Journey

Let me tell you about Lisa, a 34-year-old teacher who felt like she was "all over the place emotionally." Some days she felt confident and creative in her classroom, while other days she felt overwhelmed and wanted to hide. Her relationships were similarly inconsistent - sometimes she was warm and engaging, other times withdrawn and critical.

When Lisa started mapping her parts, she initially felt confused. "I don't know how many parts I have or what to call them," she said. So we started simple - just noticing when she felt different and jotting down a few words about each state.

Over several weeks, Lisa's map began to emerge:

Teacher Lisa showed up in the classroom and loved creating engaging lessons. This part felt confident, creative, and purposeful. Teacher Lisa had developed during Lisa's education program when she discovered she had a gift for connecting with students.

Social Chameleon appeared at parties and social gatherings, expertly reading the room and adapting to whatever energy was present. This part had learned to blend in during Lisa's awkward middle school years when standing out felt dangerous.

Perfectionist took over when Lisa was planning lessons or grading papers, setting impossibly high standards and criticizing any work that fell short. This part had formed when Lisa's parents praised her achievements but seemed disappointed when she made mistakes.

Overwhelmed Kid emerged when Lisa faced conflict or criticism, making her want to hide or cry. This part felt about eight years old and carried memories of being bullied at school with no one to help her.

Caretaker showed up in friendships, always listening to others' problems and offering support but rarely sharing her own struggles. This part had developed when Lisa's parents divorced and she learned to keep peace by taking care of everyone else's emotions.

Inner Critic provided running commentary on everything Lisa did, pointing out flaws and potential failures. This part worked closely with the Perfectionist but was much harsher, using shame and self-attack as motivational tools.

As Lisa mapped these parts, several things became clear. Her inconsistent moods made perfect sense - different situations activated different parts with different emotional signatures. Her relationship patterns reflected her parts' different strategies for connection and protection. Most importantly, she wasn't "messed up" - she was a complex person with an understandable internal system.

Common Mapping Challenges

As you work on your own map, you might run into some common obstacles:

Too Many Parts Some people worry they have too many parts. "I identified fifteen different parts - is that normal?" The answer is that there's no "right" number. Some people have a few distinct parts, others have many. What matters is understanding the ones that are most active and influential in your life.

Parts That Don't Want to Be Mapped Sometimes parts resist being identified or understood. A Secretive part might not want to be "figured out," or a Rebel part might resist any kind of categorization. If you encounter resistance, approach it with curiosity rather than force. What is the resistant part afraid will happen if it's mapped?

Parts That Change Names or Descriptions Your understanding of your parts will shift as you get to know them better. A part you initially called "Angry" might turn out to be more accurately described as "Protective." A part that felt like an adult might reveal itself to be quite young. This evolution is normal and healthy.

Overlapping or Confusing Parts Sometimes parts seem to blend together or have similar functions. You might have both a Perfectionist and a High Achiever that seem related but distinct. Don't worry about making perfect distinctions - focus on understanding the general patterns and functions.

Using Your Map

Once you have a basic map of your parts, you can start using it in practical ways:

Daily Check-Ins Throughout the day, you can ask yourself, "Which part is most active right now?" This simple question increases your self-awareness and gives you more choice about how to respond to situations.

Conflict Resolution When you feel internal conflict, you can identify which parts are disagreeing and what each one needs. Instead of feeling torn and confused, you can mediate between your parts with understanding.

Relationship Navigation Understanding your parts helps you navigate relationships more skillfully. You can recognize when a Protective part is making you defensive, or when a People-Pleasing part is overriding your authentic preferences.

Trigger Management Your map helps you understand why certain situations are particularly challenging. If you know that criticism activates your Shame-Prone part, you can prepare strategies for handling feedback more effectively.

The Evolution of Your Map

Your parts map isn't a static document - it will continue to change and develop as you grow and have new experiences. Parts that were once very active might recede into the background, while previously quiet parts might become more prominent.

Life transitions often activate new parts or change the roles of existing ones. Becoming a parent might activate nurturing parts you didn't know you had. Starting a new career might require developing parts that can handle different kinds of challenges. Going through loss or trauma might bring protective parts to the forefront while exile parts need extra care.

This evolution is normal and healthy. Your internal system is designed to adapt to changing circumstances, just like any living system.

Advanced Mapping Techniques

As you become more comfortable with basic parts mapping, you might want to explore more sophisticated techniques:

Parts Constellations Look at how your parts cluster together. You might have a "Work Cluster" that includes your Achiever, Perfectionist, and People-Pleaser parts. Or a "Relationship Cluster" that includes your Romantic, Caretaker, and Vulnerable parts. Understanding these clusters helps you see patterns in how parts activate together.

Parts Hierarchies Some parts have more influence than others in your system. Your Inner Critic might be so dominant that it affects most other parts, while your Creative part might be quite influential when it's active but often gets overruled. Mapping these power dynamics helps you understand your internal politics.

Parts Cycles Notice if your parts follow predictable patterns over time. You might have daily cycles (Anxious in the morning, Confident in the afternoon) or longer cycles (Motivated at the beginning of projects, Overwhelmed in the middle, Relief-seeking at the end).

Integration with Self-Leadership

As you develop your parts map, keep connecting with your Self-leadership. Your Self is the part of you that can hold space for all your parts without being taken over by any of them. From Self, you can appreciate each part's contributions while also providing the coordination they need to work together effectively.

Sometimes people worry that mapping their parts will make them more fragmented or "multiple." The opposite is actually true. When you understand your parts consciously, you become more integrated because you're coordinating them from Self-leadership rather than being unconsciously driven by them.

Your Mapping Practice This Week

This week, your primary task is to begin creating your own parts map. Start simple and build complexity over time. Here's what to focus on:

Daily Awareness Several times each day, pause and ask yourself:

- How am I feeling right now?
- What part of me is most active?
- What does this part care about?
- When have I felt this way before?

Keep a Parts Journal Write down your observations about different parts as you notice them. Don't worry about being systematic at first - just capture what you observe.

Name Your Major Players By the end of the week, try to identify and name 5-7 of your most active or influential parts. These might include your most common protector parts, any exile parts you've noticed, and any other parts that show up regularly in your life.

Stay Curious, Not Critical Approach this work with curiosity rather than judgment. Every part developed for good reasons, even the ones that sometimes cause problems. Your job isn't to evaluate your parts but to understand them.

Moving Forward

Next week, you'll learn about some of the most common types of parts that show up across different people's systems. This will help you refine your own map and understand that you're not alone in having certain kinds of internal conflicts or patterns.

But for now, focus on getting to know your unique internal family. Your parts have been with you your whole life, working hard to help you navigate the world. It's time to give them the recognition and understanding they deserve.

Creating a parts map is like learning the names and personalities of people you live with. Once you know who you're sharing space with, everything becomes more manageable, more interesting, and more workable.

Your internal family is unique, complex, and completely understandable. The mapping process helps you see this clearly, setting the stage for the deeper work of dialogue and integration that's coming next.

Chapter 6: Common Parts Everyone Has

Walk into any coffee shop and look around. You'll see the person frantically typing on their laptop with multiple browser tabs open - that's probably their Achiever part hard at work. There's someone carefully checking their appearance in their phone camera before taking a selfie - their Image Manager is on duty. Over in the corner, someone is scrolling through their phone instead of working on the project they brought - that could be their Procrastinator or maybe their Overwhelmed part taking a break.

While every person's internal family is unique, certain types of parts show up so frequently that they're almost universal. Understanding these common parts can help you recognize your own internal cast of characters and realize that you're not alone in having certain struggles or patterns.

These **archetypal parts** develop because humans face similar challenges across cultures and time periods. We all need to belong, stay safe, achieve goals, and protect our vulnerable aspects. The specific strategies our parts use might vary, but the underlying functions are remarkably consistent.

The Universal Protector Parts

Let's start with the most common protector parts - the ones whose job it is to keep you safe, successful, and accepted in the world.

The People-Pleaser

This might be the most common protector part of all. The People-Pleaser learned early that keeping others happy is the key to safety and acceptance. This part says yes when it wants to say no, apologizes constantly, and works overtime to make sure no one is upset or disappointed.

The People-Pleaser typically develops in families where someone's anger or disappointment felt dangerous to a young child. Maybe a parent had explosive anger, or maybe they used guilt and disappointment as forms of control. The child learned that managing other people's emotions was a matter of survival.

How to recognize your People-Pleaser:

- You automatically say "sorry" even when you didn't do anything wrong
- You feel guilty when you prioritize your own needs
- You can sense others' moods from across the room
- You change your opinions based on who you're talking to
- You feel anxious when someone seems upset, even if it has nothing to do with you

Research shows that people-pleasing behaviors often correlate with childhood emotional neglect or inconsistent (Webb, 2012; Clark, Rock, Clark, & Murray-Lyon, 2020; Evraire, Fitzpatrick, & Hewitt, 2022; Jack & Dill, 1992). The child learns to monitor and manage others' emotions as a way of ensuring their own emotional and physical safety.

The People-Pleaser's gifts: This part makes you incredibly attuned to others' needs, empathetic, and skilled at creating harmony. When it's not working overtime, it contributes to your ability to be considerate and caring.

The People-Pleaser's challenges: This part can exhaust itself trying to control others' reactions, often leading to resentment, burnout, and loss of authentic self-expression.

The Inner Critic

If the People-Pleaser is concerned with external approval, the Inner Critic is focused on internal standards. This part provides constant commentary on your performance, appearance, and worth, usually with a harsh, perfectionist edge.

The Inner Critic often develops as a way of preventing criticism from others. The logic goes: "If I criticize myself first and push myself to be perfect, then no one else can find fault with me." This part might have learned its critical voice from a harsh parent, teacher, or peer group.

How to recognize your Inner Critic:

- You have a running commentary of self-judgment in your head
- You focus on what went wrong rather than what went right
- You set impossibly high standards for yourself
- You feel like you're never good enough, no matter what you achieve
- You compare yourself constantly to others

The Inner Critic is often confused with realistic self-assessment, but there's a key difference. Realistic assessment is curious and solution-focused: "That didn't work well. What can I learn?" The Inner Critic is harsh and shaming: "You're such an idiot. You always mess things up."

The Inner Critic's gifts: This part helps you maintain standards, notice areas for improvement, and push yourself to grow. When it's not being harsh, it contributes to your ability to be discerning and self-reflective.

The Inner Critic's challenges: This part can be so harsh that it paralyzes you with shame, prevents risk-taking, and creates chronic dissatisfaction with yourself and your achievements.

The Controller

The Controller believes that if you can just manage all the variables in your environment, you can prevent bad things from happening. This part makes detailed plans, tries to anticipate every possible outcome, and gets anxious when things feel unpredictable.

Controllers often develop in chaotic or unpredictable environments where having some control felt like survival. A child who grew up with an alcoholic parent, for example, might develop a strong Controller part that tries to manage everyone and everything to prevent the chaos they experienced.

How to recognize your Controller:

- You make detailed plans and get upset when they change
- You try to manage other people's decisions and behaviors
- You feel anxious when you can't predict outcomes
- You take on more responsibility than is actually yours
- You believe that relaxing your vigilance will lead to disaster

Studies on anxiety disorders show that attempts to control uncertainty often increase anxiety rather than decrease it (Dugas & Robichaud, 2007). The more the Controller tries to eliminate uncertainty, the more threatening uncertainty becomes.

The Controller's gifts: This part helps you be organized, prepared, and responsible. It contributes to your ability to plan ahead and manage complex situations.

The Controller's challenges: This part can exhaust itself trying to control things that aren't actually controllable, leading to anxiety, rigidity, and difficulty enjoying spontaneous experiences.

The Achiever

The Achiever is driven to succeed, accomplish goals, and prove worth through performance. This part works hard, sets ambitious targets, and feels anxious when not being productive. Success equals safety in the Achiever's worldview.

Achievers often develop in families where love and attention were conditional on performance. The child learned that being successful, smart, or accomplished was the way to earn approval and avoid rejection.

How to recognize your Achiever:

- You feel guilty when you're not being productive
- Your self-worth is tied to your accomplishments
- You have trouble relaxing or taking breaks
- You set goal after goal without pausing to enjoy achievements
- You feel anxious when you're not making progress on something

The Achiever's gifts: This part gives you motivation, persistence, and the ability to turn dreams into reality. It contributes to your capacity for dedication and excellence.

The Achiever's challenges: This part can become addicted to achievement, never allowing you to rest or be satisfied with what you've accomplished. It can also make you neglect relationships and self-care in pursuit of goals.

The Caretaker

The Caretaker focuses on others' needs, problems, and wellbeing, often to the exclusion of their own. This part feels valuable when it's helping, supporting, or rescuing others. Being needed equals being loved in the Caretaker's logic.

Caretakers often develop in families where a child had to take care of adults' emotional or practical needs. This might happen when a parent is depressed, addicted, or overwhelmed, and the child learns that their worth comes from being helpful and low-maintenance.

How to recognize your Caretaker:

- You automatically offer help before being asked
- You feel uncomfortable when others try to take care of you
- You attract people who need rescuing or fixing
- You feel guilty focusing on your own needs
- You define yourself by how much you give to others

The Caretaker's gifts: This part makes you naturally giving, empathetic, and supportive. It contributes to your ability to create nurturing relationships and help others grow.

The Caretaker's challenges: This part can exhaust itself giving to others while neglecting its own needs, often leading to burnout, resentment, and relationships that feel one-sided.

Universal Exile Parts

Now let's look at some of the most common exile parts - the ones that carry your wounds, authentic feelings, and spontaneous nature.

The Wounded Child

Almost everyone has exile parts that feel young and carry early hurts. These might be specific to particular ages or experiences, but they share common characteristics: they feel vulnerable, need comfort and protection, and carry the pain of not getting what they needed when they were actually young.

How to recognize your Wounded Child:

- Certain situations make you feel suddenly much younger than your actual age
- You have disproportionate emotional reactions to rejection or criticism

- You long for someone to take care of you, even though you're capable of taking care of yourself

- You feel hurt when others don't notice your needs without being told

- You sometimes feel like you're still that scared/sad/angry kid inside

The Wounded Child's gifts: This part carries your capacity for wonder, trust, and authentic emotion. When it feels safe, it contributes spontaneity, creativity, and the ability to love openly.

The Wounded Child's challenges: When this part is activated, you might react from old wounds rather than current reality, leading to behaviors that don't fit your adult life.

The Angry Kid

Many people have an exile part that carries legitimate anger about unfair treatment, boundary violations, or injustice. This part might have been told that anger was bad, dangerous, or unacceptable, so it went into hiding but continues to carry the fire of righteous indignation.

How to recognize your Angry Kid:

- You have sudden flashes of intense anger that seem bigger than the current situation

- You feel guilty or scared when you get angry

- You attract people who walk all over you, then explode unexpectedly

- You have fantasies of telling people exactly what you think of them

- You swing between being overly accommodating and being furious

The Angry Kid's gifts: This part carries your sense of justice, your ability to set boundaries, and your capacity to stand up for yourself and others.

The Angry Kid's challenges: When this part has been suppressed for too long, it might explode inappropriately or turn its anger inward as depression.

The Creative Dreamer

Most people have an exile part that carries their artistic impulses, big dreams, and imaginative nature. This part often gets exiled when families or schools emphasize "being realistic" over creativity and wonder.

How to recognize your Creative Dreamer:

- You have artistic impulses that you dismiss as impractical
- You feel guilty spending time on creative activities that don't "produce" anything
- You have big dreams that you're afraid to pursue
- You feel alive when you're being creative but tell yourself it's not important
- You admire creative people but think you could never be like them

The Creative Dreamer's gifts: This part carries your imagination, artistic ability, and connection to beauty and meaning.

The Creative Dreamer's challenges: When this part is exiled, you might feel like something essential is missing from your life, even if everything else looks successful.

Firefighter Parts

There's another category of parts that IFS calls "firefighters" - parts that emerge in crisis situations or when exile parts are in pain. These parts often use more extreme strategies to cope with overwhelming situations.

The Rebel

The Rebel emerges when other strategies aren't working or when you feel trapped or controlled. This part might break rules, act out, or do the opposite of what's expected as a way of asserting independence or expressing protest.

How to recognize your Rebel:

- You have impulses to do the opposite of what you're "supposed" to do
- You feel claustrophobic when people have expectations of you
- You sometimes sabotage your own success when it starts feeling too controlled
- You're attracted to rule-breaking or non-conformist behavior
- You feel energized by going against the grain

The Rebel's gifts: This part protects your autonomy, authenticity, and freedom. It prevents you from becoming completely domesticated or losing your individual spirit.

The Rebel's challenges: This part can sabotage your goals and relationships when it reacts against healthy structure or commitment.

The Escape Artist

When life feels too overwhelming, the Escape Artist looks for ways to check out temporarily. This might be through substances, addictive behaviors, fantasy, sleep, or any activity that provides relief from difficult feelings or situations.

How to recognize your Escape Artist:

- You have go-to activities that help you "disappear" from stress
- You sometimes lose hours to mindless activities (scrolling, gaming, watching TV)
- You use substances, food, shopping, or other behaviors to change how you feel
- You fantasize about running away or starting a completely new life
- You feel guilty about your escape behaviors but can't seem to stop them

The Escape Artist's gifts: This part provides necessary breaks from overwhelming stress and helps you cope when you don't have other resources available.

The Escape Artist's challenges: This part can become problematic when escape becomes the primary coping strategy, interfering with responsibilities and relationships.

How These Parts Interact

Understanding common parts is helpful, but what's more important is understanding how your specific parts relate to each other. Most internal conflict comes from parts with different strategies trying to help you at the same time.

For example:

- Your Achiever wants to work late to finish a project, while your Caretaker thinks you should spend time with your family
- Your People-Pleaser says yes to a social invitation, while your Introvert part needs alone time to recharge
- Your Controller tries to plan every detail of a vacation, while your Spontaneous part wants to leave room for adventure

- Your Inner Critic attacks your Creative Dreamer for "wasting time" on artistic projects

These conflicts aren't character flaws - they're natural tensions between parts with different values and strategies. The key is learning to mediate between your parts from Self-leadership rather than being caught in the middle of their disagreements.

Cultural Variations

While certain parts are nearly universal, the specific ways they develop and express themselves can vary significantly based on cultural background, family patterns, and individual experiences.

In cultures that emphasize individual achievement, you might see more developed Achiever and Controller parts. In cultures that prioritize harmony and collective wellbeing, People-Pleaser and Caretaker parts might be more prominent.

Family dynamics also shape how parts develop. In families where emotions are freely expressed, Angry parts might be more integrated. In families where emotions are suppressed, those same parts might become exiles.

This doesn't mean some cultural patterns are better than others - just that understanding your cultural context can help you understand why certain parts developed more strongly in your system.

Working with Common Parts

Recognizing these common parts in yourself can be both relieving and overwhelming. Relieving because you realize you're not uniquely messed up - millions of people have similar internal patterns. Overwhelming because you might suddenly see parts everywhere and feel like you don't know who you "really" are.

Here are some guidelines for working with common parts:

Normalize, don't pathologize: Having a strong Inner Critic or People-Pleaser doesn't make you damaged. These are normal responses to life circumstances.

Appreciate their intentions: Every part developed to help you, even if their strategies no longer serve you well.

Don't try to eliminate parts: The goal isn't to get rid of parts but to help them work together more effectively.

Focus on the most active parts: You don't need to work with every part at once. Start with the ones that have the biggest impact on your daily life.

Stay connected to Self: Remember that understanding your parts is meant to increase your Self-leadership, not fragment you further.

Your Common Parts This Week

This week, use the descriptions in this chapter to refine your parts map. See which of these common parts resonate with your experience and which ones don't seem relevant to your system.

Pay attention to:

- Which common parts you recognized immediately in yourself
- Any parts you have that seem different from the ones described here
- How your parts might be influenced by your cultural or family background
- Interactions between your parts that create internal conflict

Don't worry if you don't relate to all the parts described or if your parts seem to work differently. These are general patterns, not rigid categories. Your internal family is uniquely yours, even if it shares some common characteristics with others.

Understanding Your Uniqueness

While common parts can help you recognize patterns in your own system, what makes your internal family special is how these parts combine, interact, and express themselves in your particular life.

Your People-Pleaser might be gentle and accommodating, while someone else's might be anxious and controlling. Your Inner Critic might focus on work performance, while another person's might be obsessed with appearance. Your Creative Dreamer might express through music, while someone else's might be focused on business innovation.

The goal of understanding common parts isn't to put yourself in a box, but to give you a starting point for understanding your own unique internal system.

Next week, you'll learn more about how parts interact and create the complex patterns of internal conflict and cooperation that shape your daily experience. Understanding these dynamics is key to becoming a more skilled leader of your internal family.

Chapter 7: How Parts Interact and Conflict

Think about the last time you were at a family dinner where different relatives had strong opinions about something controversial. Maybe Uncle Bob started talking politics while Aunt Sarah tried to change the subject, your teenage cousin rolled their eyes and put in earbuds, and your mom frantically offered everyone more food to distract from the tension.

That chaotic family dinner? That's what's happening inside your head most of the time.

Your parts don't exist in isolation - they're constantly interacting, negotiating, competing for influence, and sometimes flat-out arguing with each other. Understanding these **internal dynamics** is crucial because most of your emotional struggles come not from individual parts, but from the conflicts between them.

When you feel paralyzed by a decision, it's usually because two or more parts want different things and can't agree. When you feel "torn" or "conflicted," you're literally experiencing parts that are pulling you in different directions. When you do something and then immediately regret it, one part probably took action while another part disagreed with the choice.

The Internal Family Dynamics

Just like biological families, your internal family has complex relationships, alliances, power struggles, and patterns that have developed over years or decades. Some parts work together beautifully, others barely tolerate each other, and some are in active warfare.

Understanding these dynamics helps explain why changing patterns can be so difficult. It's not just about willpower or motivation - it's about mediating between parts that have different agendas, different fears, and different strategies for keeping you safe and successful.

Parts Alliances Some of your parts work together as a team. Your Achiever and your Perfectionist might partner up to help you succeed at work. Your People-Pleaser and your Caretaker might join forces to make sure everyone around you is happy and taken care of. Your Creative Dreamer and your Rebel might collaborate to help you break free from conventional expectations.

These alliances can be powerful and productive when they're serving your overall wellbeing. But they can also gang up on other parts, creating internal oppression. If your Achiever and Perfectionist team up against your Fun-Loving part, you might find it impossible to relax or play.

Parts Opposition Other parts seem to be in direct opposition to each other. Your Controller wants to plan everything in advance, while your Spontaneous part wants to be open to whatever emerges. Your People-Pleaser wants to say yes to every request, while your Boundary-Setter wants to protect your time and energy.

This opposition isn't necessarily bad - it can create healthy internal checks and balances. The problem arises when opposing parts can't communicate effectively, leading to internal stalemates or flip-flopping between extremes.

Parts Hierarchies In most internal systems, some parts have more influence or power than others. Your Inner Critic might be so dominant that it influences most of your other parts' behavior. Or your People-Pleaser might be so strong that it overrides your authentic preferences most of the time (Anderson, & Sweezy 2017).

These hierarchies often reflect your life history. Parts that helped you survive difficult early experiences often maintain positions of power even when their strategies are no longer needed. A Controller part that developed during childhood chaos might still be running the show in your stable adult life.

Common Conflict Patterns

Let's look at some of the most frequent types of internal conflicts and how they play out:

The Push-Pull Dynamic

This happens when you have parts that want opposite things, creating a constant internal tug-of-war. Common examples include:

Independence vs. Connection Your Independent part values freedom and self-reliance, while your Connection-Seeking part wants closeness and intimacy. In relationships, this might show up as alternating between clinging and distancing - getting close to someone, then pulling away when it feels too intense, then feeling lonely and moving closer again.

Marcus experienced this pattern in his romantic relationships. His Independent part had learned to rely only on himself after his parents' bitter divorce. This part valued his freedom and was suspicious of anyone who might limit his choices. But he also had a Connection-Seeking part that longed for deep intimacy and partnership.

In relationships, Marcus would start strong, enjoying the closeness and connection. But as things got more serious, his Independent part would get nervous and start finding reasons to create distance. This would trigger his Connection-Seeking part, which would then work overtime to repair the relationship. The cycle would repeat until either Marcus or his partner got exhausted by the inconsistency.

Achievement vs. Rest Your Achiever wants to constantly work and improve, while your Rest-Seeking part needs downtime and recovery. This creates internal conflict around productivity, self-care, and work-life balance.

Sarah found herself caught in this conflict daily. Her Achiever part had been shaped by parents who praised hard work and achievement above all else. This part felt guilty whenever Sarah wasn't being productive and drove her to work long hours and take on extra projects.

But Sarah also had a Rest-Seeking part that was exhausted from years of overwork. This part would try to assert itself by making Sarah feel too tired to concentrate or by creating mild illnesses that forced her to slow down. The two parts were locked in a battle that left Sarah feeling either guilty (when she rested) or exhausted (when she pushed through).

The Protective vs. Exile Dynamic

This is one of the most important patterns to understand. Your protector parts often work overtime to keep your exile parts hidden and safe. But exile parts need expression and attention, creating ongoing internal tension.

The Perfectionist vs. The Creative Child Your Perfectionist protector might shut down your Creative Child exile because creativity involves risk, messiness, and potential criticism. The Perfectionist learned that perfect performance equals safety, while the Creative Child just wants to play and explore.

Jennifer was a successful marketing executive whose Perfectionist part had helped her climb the corporate ladder. This part ensured that every presentation was flawless, every email was carefully crafted, and every project exceeded expectations.

But Jennifer also had a Creative Child part that had loved art and writing as a young person. This part had been gradually shut down as Jennifer learned to focus on "practical" skills. The Creative Child would occasionally surface, filling Jennifer with longing to take a pottery class or write poetry. But the Perfectionist would quickly intervene, pointing out that these activities were "wastes of time" that wouldn't advance her career.

The conflict between these parts left Jennifer feeling successful but empty, accomplished but disconnected from what brought her joy.

The Controller vs. The Vulnerable Child Your Controller protector tries to manage outcomes and prevent unpredictability, while your Vulnerable Child exile needs to feel safe being dependent and open to others' care.

David's Controller part had developed during his chaotic childhood with an alcoholic father. This part learned to anticipate problems, manage crises, and never count on others for important needs. As an adult, David's Controller helped him be successful at work and manage complex projects.

But David also had a Vulnerable Child part that longed to be taken care of, to lean on others, and to trust that people would be there for him. This part would emerge in romantic relationships, wanting David's partner to anticipate his needs and provide comfort and reassurance.

The Controller part saw the Vulnerable Child as dangerous - if David let himself depend on others, he might get hurt the way he did as a child. So the Controller would work to shut down vulnerability, making David appear completely self-sufficient even when he was struggling.

The Manager vs. Firefighter Dynamic

This happens when your everyday manager parts (like the Responsible Adult or the People-Pleaser) conflict with your emergency firefighter parts (like the Rebel or the Escape Artist).

Manager parts try to keep things stable and predictable, following rules and meeting expectations. Firefighter parts emerge when the system feels overwhelmed or when exile parts are in pain, using more extreme strategies to cope or rebel.

Lisa experienced this as the "good girl gone wild" pattern. Most of the time, her Manager parts kept her responsible, reliable, and pleasing to authority figures. She showed up on time, met her obligations, and rarely caused problems.

But when Lisa felt too controlled or when her authentic self felt completely suppressed, her Rebel firefighter would take over. She might quit her job impulsively, end a relationship dramatically, or make other sudden changes that her Manager parts would later regret.

The cycle would repeat: Manager parts would reassert control, keeping Lisa "good" until the pressure built up again and the Rebel would explode into action.

How Conflicts Develop

Parts conflicts don't happen randomly - they develop for specific reasons:

Incompatible Survival Strategies Different parts might have learned conflicting strategies for staying safe or getting needs met. Your People-Pleaser learned that keeping others happy equals safety, while your Authentic Self knows that constant people-pleasing leads to disconnection from your true nature.

Developmental Timing Parts that developed at different ages might have different levels of sophistication or different understandings of current reality. Your Adult Protector knows that making mistakes is part of learning, while your Young Perfectionist is still operating from the belief that any mistake could lead to rejection or punishment.

Conflicting Values Sometimes parts conflict because they hold genuinely different values. Your Family-Oriented part values loyalty and togetherness, while your Individual Growth part values personal development and independence. Both values are legitimate, but they can pull you in different directions.

Resource Competition Parts might compete for limited resources like time, energy, or attention. Your Work part wants you to focus on career advancement, while your Relationship part wants you to invest in personal connections. Your Self-Care part needs rest and recovery, while your Achievement part wants to use every moment productively.

The Consequences of Unresolved Conflict

When parts conflicts go unresolved, they can create significant problems:

Decision Paralysis When parts can't agree on what to do, you might find yourself unable to make decisions, even about relatively small things. You research endlessly, make pros and cons lists, ask everyone for advice, but can't move forward because different parts want different outcomes.

Flip-Flopping Behavior You might make decisions based on whichever part is strongest in the moment, then change your mind when another part takes over. This can look like inconsistency or unreliability to others, but it's actually parts taking turns running the show.

Self-Sabotage Sometimes parts conflicts lead to self-sabotaging behavior. One part works toward a goal while another part unconsciously undermines the effort. You might work hard to lose weight while also finding yourself eating late at night, or put effort into improving a relationship while also picking fights.

Emotional Overwhelm Unresolved parts conflicts can create intense emotional states. You might feel simultaneously angry and guilty, excited and terrified, or loving and resentful. These mixed emotions can be confusing and exhausting.

Physical Symptoms Parts conflicts often show up in the body as tension, headaches, digestive issues, or other stress-related symptoms. Your system is literally pulling itself in different directions.

Mediating Between Parts

The key to resolving parts conflicts isn't to pick a winner, but to help your parts communicate and find solutions that work for everyone. This requires Self-leadership - the ability to understand all perspectives without being taken over by any of them.

Step 1: Recognize the Conflict Instead of feeling confused or overwhelmed, identify that you have parts in disagreement. "I'm not just conflicted - I have a part that wants to take this job and another part that's scared of the responsibility."

Step 2: Give Each Part a Voice Listen to what each part is trying to accomplish. What is each part afraid will happen if the other part gets its way? What does each part need to feel heard and valued?

Step 3: Look for Creative Solutions From Self-leadership, you can often find solutions that honor multiple parts' needs. Maybe your Social part can have connection time while your Introvert part gets the alone time it needs. Maybe your Achiever part can pursue goals in ways that don't exhaust your Rest-Seeking part.

Step 4: Negotiate Timing Sometimes parts can take turns rather than fighting for constant control. Your Responsible part can handle work hours while your Playful part gets evenings and weekends. Your People-Pleaser can show up in some relationships while your Boundary-Setter protects your limits in others.

James's Internal Mediation

James was torn between two job offers - one with a prestigious company that would advance his career, and another with a non-profit that aligned with his values but paid less money. Instead of agonizing over the decision, James decided to explore which parts were involved in the conflict.

His Achiever part was excited about the prestigious job. This part had worked hard to build James's career and saw this as the natural next step. The Achiever was afraid that taking the lower-paying job would mean wasting all the effort that had gone into building professional credentials.

His Values-Driven part was drawn to the non-profit work. This part cared deeply about making a meaningful contribution to the world and felt energized by work that aligned with James's core beliefs. This part was afraid that taking the corporate job would mean selling out and losing connection to what really mattered.

James also discovered a Security-Seeking part that was worried about money. This part had developed during James's childhood when his family struggled financially, and it equated higher salary with safety and stability.

Instead of letting these parts battle it out, James facilitated a conversation between them. The Achiever acknowledged that career advancement wasn't worth sacrificing James's sense of purpose. The Values-Driven part understood that financial security was important for James's overall wellbeing. The Security-Seeking part recognized that James had skills and experience that would create opportunities regardless of which job he chose.

Together, the parts agreed that James should take the non-profit job for two years to satisfy his Values-Driven part, while actively building skills and connections that would serve his Achiever part's long-term goals. The Security-Seeking part felt better knowing that James would be building his resume even while earning less money initially.

Your Parts Conflicts This Week

This week, focus on identifying and understanding the conflicts between your parts. Pay attention to:

Decision struggles: When you can't decide what to do, ask yourself which parts want different outcomes.

Mixed emotions: When you feel several conflicting emotions at once, see if you can identify which parts are active.

Self-sabotage: If you find yourself working against your own stated goals, look for parts that might disagree with those goals.

Flip-flopping: When you change your mind frequently, notice if different parts are taking turns influencing your decisions.

Body tension: Physical tension often reflects parts pulling in different directions.

The goal isn't to resolve all your parts conflicts immediately, but to start recognizing them as parts conflicts rather than personal failings or character flaws.

Moving Toward Integration

Understanding how your parts interact and conflict is the foundation for helping them work together more effectively. Instead of being caught in the middle of internal battles, you can become a skilled mediator who helps different aspects of yourself coordinate their efforts.

This doesn't mean eliminating conflict entirely - some creative tension between parts can be productive. But it does mean moving from unconscious internal warfare to conscious internal collaboration.

Next week, you'll learn about blended states - what happens when parts take over so completely that you temporarily lose access to your Self-leadership. Understanding blending is crucial for reclaiming your ability to choose how you respond to life's challenges.

Your internal family conflicts aren't signs of psychological problems - they're natural tensions between different aspects of yourself that want to help you in different ways. With skillful Self-leadership, these conflicts can become sources of creativity, balance, and wisdom.

Chapter 8: Recognizing Blended States

Have you ever had the experience of saying something in an argument and thinking, "That didn't sound like me at all"? Or maybe you've looked back on a decision you made and wondered, "What was I thinking?" Or perhaps you've had moments where you felt completely overwhelmed by emotions that seemed way too big for the situation.

If so, you've experienced what IFS calls **blending** - when a part takes over so completely that you temporarily lose access to your Self-leadership. Instead of having a part (like having an angry reaction), you become the part (like being totally consumed by rage).

Blending is one of the most important concepts to understand in IFS work because it explains why you sometimes feel like a different person in different situations, why you might make decisions you later regret, and why changing certain patterns can feel so difficult.

When you're blended, you're not thinking from your calm, wise Self - you're thinking from the perspective of whichever part has taken over. This part's view of the world becomes your view of the world, at least temporarily.

What Blending Looks and Feels Like

Blending can be dramatic and obvious, or it can be subtle and hard to detect. Here are some signs that you might be blended with a part:

Your perspective narrows suddenly. When you're in Self-leadership, you can usually see multiple sides of a situation. When you're blended, you can only see things from one part's point of view. Your usually reasonable friend becomes "totally unreasonable" when your Defensive part is blended. Your normally manageable job becomes "absolutely impossible" when your Overwhelmed part takes over.

Your emotional reactions feel disproportionate. A minor criticism triggers shame that feels devastating. A small delay creates anxiety that feels catastrophic. A friend's success generates envy that feels consuming. The emotion is much bigger than what the current situation would typically warrant.

You lose access to your usual coping skills. Normally you might be able to take deep breaths when stressed, but when your Panic part is blended, breathing techniques seem impossible or stupid. Usually you can see your partner's point of view during disagreements, but when your Defensive part takes over, they seem like the enemy.

You make decisions that your Self later questions. You send an angry email that you immediately regret. You agree to commitments that overwhelm your schedule. You quit a job impulsively or end a relationship dramatically. Later, when you're not blended, you wonder why you made that choice.

You feel like you're not quite yourself. There's a sense that "this isn't really me" or "I don't know where that came from." You might feel like you're watching yourself from outside, or like someone else is driving your behavior.

Your body language and voice change. When different parts blend, you might notice changes in your posture, facial expressions, or tone of voice. Your Confident part might make you stand taller, while your Insecure part makes you hunch your shoulders. Your People-Pleaser might make your voice softer, while your Angry part makes it sharper.

Types of Blending

Blending can happen in different ways and to different degrees:

Sudden Blending This is the most obvious type - when a part takes over quickly and dramatically. You're having a normal conversation with your partner when they mention something that triggers your Abandoned Child part, and suddenly you're sobbing and saying things like, "You never really loved me anyway."

Rachel experienced sudden blending during a work meeting when her boss mentioned that the team needed to "step up their game." Rachel's Criticized Child part, which carried memories of harsh judgment from her father, immediately took over. Within seconds, Rachel went from feeling confident and engaged to feeling worthless and defensive. She spent the rest of the meeting convinced that she was about to be fired, even though her boss's comment wasn't directed at her specifically.

Gradual Blending Sometimes parts take over slowly, like a tide rolling in. You might not notice at first, but gradually you realize you've been completely consumed by worry, criticism, or some other part-driven state.

David noticed this pattern with his Controller part. During stressful periods, this part would gradually take more and more control over his life. First, David would start making more detailed to-do lists. Then he'd begin micromanaging his family's schedules. Eventually, he'd be trying to control every aspect of his environment, feeling anxious whenever anything unpredictable happened. The blending was so gradual that David often didn't realize how controlling he'd become until someone pointed it out.

Chronic Blending Sometimes parts stay blended for long periods - weeks, months, or even years. You might be so identified with a particular part that you think it's just "who you are." Someone might be chronically blended with their People-Pleaser part and think they're just "naturally" considerate. Another person might be chronically blended with their Inner Critic and believe they're just "realistic" about their flaws.

Maria had been chronically blended with her Responsible Adult part for so long that she'd forgotten she had other aspects to her personality. This part had taken over when Maria was twelve and her mother became seriously ill. Maria learned to manage the household, care for her younger siblings, and handle adult responsibilities.

Twenty years later, Maria was still completely identified with being responsible. She couldn't relax, couldn't play, and couldn't let anyone else take care of anything important. When friends suggested she "just have fun," Maria literally couldn't understand what they meant. Fun felt foreign and irresponsible. Maria wasn't accessing her Responsible part when needed - she was permanently blended with it.

Why Blending Happens

Understanding why blending occurs can help you respond to it with more compassion and skill:

Overwhelming Triggers Sometimes parts blend because they're triggered by something that feels emotionally overwhelming. A criticism that reminds your inner system of childhood humiliation, a rejection that activates old abandonment wounds, or a failure that triggers deep shame. The triggered part floods the system in an attempt to protect you from re-experiencing that pain.

Lack of Self-Leadership When you're stressed, tired, or overwhelmed, your capacity for Self-leadership decreases. Parts that are usually well-coordinated by your Self might take over when your Self is depleted. This is why you might be more reactive when you're hungry, exhausted, or dealing with multiple stressors.

Parts That Don't Trust Self Some parts, especially those that developed during trauma or in chaotic environments, might not trust that your Self can handle difficult situations. These parts take over preemptively, believing that their specific expertise is required for survival.

Unmet Parts Needs Sometimes parts blend because their needs haven't been acknowledged or met for too long. A Creative part that's been ignored might take over with sudden impulses to quit your day job and become an artist. A Social part that's been suppressed might blend and create intense loneliness or social neediness.

The Consequences of Blending

While blending is natural and sometimes necessary, chronic or frequent blending can create problems:

Relationship Difficulties When you're blended, you're not relating from your whole Self - you're relating from one part's perspective. This can create confusion for others who feel like they're dealing with different people at different times. Your partner might feel like they never know "which you" they're going to encounter.

Poor Decision Making Parts have specific concerns and limited perspectives. When you make important decisions while blended, you're not considering all the relevant factors. You might make choices that serve one part's needs while ignoring other important aspects of your life.

Lost Self-Agency When parts are frequently blended, you might feel like you're not in control of your own life. You're being driven by parts' reactions rather than choosing how to respond from your Self.

Emotional Instability If different parts are taking over throughout the day, your emotional experience might feel chaotic and unpredictable. You might feel like you're on an emotional roller coaster without understanding why.

Recognizing When You're Blended

The first step in working with blending is learning to recognize when it's happening. This can be challenging because when you're blended, the part's perspective feels completely true and reasonable.

Here are some questions to ask yourself:

- Does my emotional reaction feel proportionate to what's actually happening?
- Can I see other perspectives on this situation, or does one view feel completely true?
- Do I have access to my usual coping skills and wisdom?
- Does this feel like my whole Self responding, or like one aspect of me has taken over?

- Am I able to be curious about what's happening, or do I feel certain about my interpretation?

Sometimes it's easier to recognize blending after the fact. You might look back on a situation and think, "I was so convinced that my friend was trying to hurt me, but now I can see they were just having a bad day."

Common Blending Patterns

Different people have different patterns of blending based on their life history and which parts are most active in their system:

The Perfectionist Takeover When your Perfectionist part blends, everything must be flawless. A small mistake feels catastrophic, and you can't see the bigger picture or remember that "good enough" is often sufficient. You might spend hours perfecting something that doesn't require perfection, or become paralyzed by the fear of making any errors.

The People-Pleaser Override When this part blends, other people's needs become the only consideration. Your own preferences, boundaries, and wellbeing disappear from awareness. You might agree to things that exhaust you or compromise your values because someone else's happiness feels like the only thing that matters.

The Inner Critic Attack When your Inner Critic blends, you become convinced that you're fundamentally flawed, inadequate, or failing. You can't access your strengths, accomplishments, or the love others have for you. Everything becomes evidence of your unworthiness.

The Abandoned Child Emergency When this part blends, any sign of distance or rejection feels life-threatening. Your partner being quiet triggers certainty that they're going to leave. A friend not responding to a text immediately means they don't care about you anymore. The fear feels urgent and completely justified.

Unblending Techniques

Learning to unblend - to create some space between you and the part that's taken over - is one of the most practical skills you can develop. Here are several techniques that can help:

The Pause Practice When you notice you might be blended, pause whatever you're doing. Take three deep breaths. This simple action can create enough space for your Self to come back online, even briefly.

Name the Part Instead of thinking "I am furious," try thinking "My Angry part is furious." Instead of "I'm worthless," try "My Inner Critic is telling me I'm worthless." This simple language shift can create distance between you and the part.

Ask for Space Internally, you can ask the blended part to give you some room. "Hey, Anxious part, I can see you're really worried about this presentation. Can you step back a little so I can think clearly?" Many parts will respond to respectful requests for space.

Ground in Your Body Physical grounding can help you reconnect with your Self. Feel your feet on the ground, notice your breathing, or do some gentle stretching. Parts often live in your head, while Self includes your whole being.

Look for Self-Qualities Ask yourself if you can access any curiosity, compassion, or calmness about the situation. If you can find even a little bit of these Self-qualities, you can work from there to get more space from the blended part.

Time and Space Sometimes the most effective unblending technique is simply removing yourself from the triggering situation. Go for a walk, take a bath, or find a quiet space where you can reconnect with your Self without external pressures.

Jennifer's Blending Pattern

Jennifer had a pattern of blending with her Perfectionist part during important work presentations. As soon as she stood up to speak, this part would take over completely, convinced that any mistake would be catastrophic for her career.

When blended, Jennifer couldn't access her natural speaking abilities, her sense of humor, or her ability to connect with her audience. Instead, she would deliver perfectly prepared but robotic presentations that didn't showcase her actual skills and personality.

Jennifer learned to recognize the early signs of this blending - a particular kind of anxiety that felt different from normal pre-presentation nerves. When she noticed these signs, she would:

1. **Take a bathroom break** to remove herself from the triggering environment
2. **Breathe deeply** and feel her feet on the ground
3. **Talk to her Perfectionist part**: "I know you want this presentation to go well. I want that too. But when you take over completely, we don't actually perform as well as we could."
4. **Ask for collaboration rather than takeover**: "Can you help me be prepared and professional while still letting me be natural and engaging?"
5. **Connect with her Self-qualities** by remembering what she genuinely wanted to share with her audience

This practice helped Jennifer give presentations that were both well-prepared and authentic, showcasing her actual abilities rather than just her Perfectionist part's rigid strategies.

Working with Chronic Blending

Some parts have been blended for so long that unblending feels dangerous or impossible. These parts might believe that letting go of control will lead to disaster, or they might be so used to running the show that they don't know how to step back.

Working with chronic blending often requires:

Building Self-Leadership gradually: Strengthening your capacity to stay present and centered in low-stakes situations before trying to address high-stakes blending.

Negotiating with parts: Rather than trying to force chronically blended parts to step back, you can negotiate about when their expertise is needed versus when other parts or Self-qualities might be more helpful.

Addressing underlying fears: Chronically blended parts often have deep fears about what will happen if they're not in control. These fears need to be understood and addressed before the part can relax its grip.

Getting support: Sometimes chronically blended parts need the reassurance that comes from having other people (therapists, friends, family members) who can provide stability while the part learns to trust Self-leadership.

Your Blending Awareness This Week

This week, focus on developing awareness of your own blending patterns. Pay attention to:

Triggers: What situations, people, or circumstances tend to trigger blending in your system?

Early warning signs: What are the first signals that a part might be taking over? Changes in your body, shifts in your thinking, or alterations in your emotional state?

Specific parts: Which of your parts are most prone to blending? Your Inner Critic? Your People-Pleaser? Your Anxious part?

Recovery time: How long does it typically take you to unblend naturally? What helps you reconnect with your Self-leadership?

Don't try to prevent blending entirely - it's a natural part of how internal systems work. Instead, focus on recognizing it more quickly and developing skills for unblending when it's not serving you.

Integration and Balance

The goal isn't to eliminate blending completely, but to have more choice about when it happens and more skill in unblending when necessary. Sometimes temporary blending can actually be helpful - your Focused part might blend to help you meet an important deadline, or your Protective part might blend to help you get out of a dangerous situation.

The key is developing the ability to recognize when you're blended and to consciously choose whether that's how you want to be responding in that moment.

Understanding blending is crucial for the deeper IFS work you'll be doing in the coming weeks. When you can recognize blending and maintain more consistent access to your Self-leadership, you'll be able to dialogue with your parts, negotiate between them, and help them coordinate their efforts more effectively.

Your parts aren't trying to take over to cause problems - they're usually trying to help or protect you. Learning to work with blending compassionately creates the foundation for a more collaborative relationship with all aspects of yourself.

Completing Your System Map

Congratulations on finishing the mapping phase of your IFS journey! Over these past two weeks, you've gained invaluable insight into your internal world. You've learned to identify your unique constellation of parts, understand how they developed, and recognize the complex ways they interact with each other.

You now have tools for recognizing when different parts are active, when they're in conflict, and when they've blended so completely that you've temporarily lost access to your Self-leadership. This awareness alone will begin to change your relationship with yourself, giving you more choice and less confusion about your internal experiences.

The mapping phase is foundational to everything that follows. You can't effectively work with parts you don't recognize or understand. You can't mediate conflicts between parts whose needs and fears you haven't identified. You can't maintain Self-leadership if you can't tell the difference between Self and parts.

As you move into the next phase - learning to dialogue with and heal your parts - carry with you the spirit of curiosity and compassion that makes mapping effective. Your parts aren't problems to be solved but aspects of yourself to be understood and appreciated.

Next week, you'll begin the heart of IFS work: learning to have actual conversations with your parts. This is where mapping transforms from intellectual understanding into lived relationship, where you move from knowing about your parts to actually working with them as allies in creating the life you want.

Your internal family is complex, intelligent, and ultimately workable. The mapping you've done has created the foundation for true internal collaboration. The journey continues.

Section III: Dialogue and Healing (Weeks 5-6)

Chapter 9: How to Talk to Your Parts

You've been having conversations with your parts your entire life. The only difference is that most of these conversations have been unconscious, one-sided, or adversarial. Your Inner Critic talks AT you constantly, telling you what's wrong and what you should do better. Your Anxious part floods you with worry without waiting for a response. Your People-Pleaser makes decisions for you without consulting your actual preferences.

But what if you could turn these monologues into actual dialogues? What if instead of being talked to, controlled, or overwhelmed by your parts, you could have genuine conversations with them - the kind where both sides listen and respond?

This is exactly what **parts dialogue** makes possible. It's one of the most practical and powerful tools in IFS work because it transforms your relationship with yourself from internal warfare into internal collaboration.

The idea might sound strange at first. "Talk to my parts? Like having conversations with voices in my head?" It's not about hearing literal voices or developing multiple personalities. It's about creating conscious communication with aspects of yourself that are already influencing your thoughts, feelings, and behaviors.

Think of it this way: you already have an Inner Critic that comments on your performance. Instead of just listening to its harsh judgments, what if you could ask it questions? "What are you worried will happen if I'm not perfect?" "What would help you feel less anxious about my performance?"

You already have parts that get triggered in relationships. Instead of just being swept away by their reactions, what if you could understand what they're experiencing? "Part that gets upset when my partner seems distant - what does that distance remind you of?" "What would help you feel more secure in this relationship?"

The Foundation of Parts Dialogue

Effective parts dialogue rests on several key principles that distinguish it from other forms of internal communication:

Self-Leadership The most important prerequisite for parts dialogue is accessing your Self-leadership. You can't have effective conversations with your parts while blended with other parts. Your Self needs to be the one initiating and maintaining the dialogue.

This means that if you're completely taken over by anxiety, you probably can't have a productive conversation with your Anxious part in that moment. You need to unblend first, access some Self-qualities like curiosity and compassion, and then engage with the part from that more spacious place.

Genuine Curiosity Parts dialogue isn't about manipulating your parts into behaving differently. It's about genuinely wanting to understand their experience, their concerns, and their perspective. Parts can tell the difference between authentic curiosity and attempts to control or fix them.

This curiosity needs to be non-judgmental. You're not trying to determine whether your part is right or wrong, reasonable or unreasonable. You're simply trying to understand what it's like to be that part.

Respectful Communication You would never build a good relationship with another person by being dismissive, impatient, or controlling. The same is true for your parts. Effective dialogue requires treating your parts with the same respect you would show to other people whose feelings and perspectives matter to you.

This means no internal eye-rolling when your Anxious part shares its worries, no dismissing your Creative part's dreams as "unrealistic," and no trying to shut down your Angry part because its feelings are inconvenient.

Getting Started with Parts Dialogue

If you're new to parts dialogue, the process might feel awkward or artificial at first. That's completely normal. Like any new communication skill, it takes practice to feel natural and effective.

Step 1: Create the Right Conditions Find a quiet space where you won't be interrupted. Some people like to dialogue with parts through writing, others prefer internal conversation, and still others find it helpful to speak out loud. Experiment to see what works best for you.

Make sure you're not blended with any parts that might interfere with the dialogue. If you're feeling overwhelmed, anxious, or reactive, take some time to settle into Self-leadership before beginning.

Step 2: Identify the Part You Want to Talk With Start with a part that's been active recently or one that you're curious about. It's often easier to begin with protector parts rather than exile parts, since protectors are usually more accessible and less vulnerable.

You might choose to dialogue with:

- Your Inner Critic after it's been particularly harsh
- Your People-Pleaser when you've been feeling resentful about overcommitting
- Your Controller when you've been feeling anxious about uncertainty
- Your Perfectionist when you've been procrastinating or feeling overwhelmed

Step 3: Make Contact Reach out to the part with genuine curiosity and respect. You might say something like:

- "Inner Critic part, I've noticed you've been really active lately, and I'm curious about what's going on with you."

- "People-Pleaser, I can see you've been working really hard to keep everyone happy. I'd like to understand more about what that's like for you."
- "Anxious part, you seem really worried about this upcoming presentation. I want to hear what your concerns are."

Step 4: Listen Without Trying to Fix This is often the hardest part for beginners. When your part shares its concerns, fears, or pain, resist the urge to immediately reassure, argue, or problem-solve. Just listen and acknowledge what you're hearing.

Instead of jumping in with solutions, try responses like:

- "That sounds really scary."
- "I can understand why you'd be worried about that."
- "It makes sense that you'd feel that way, given what happened before."
- "Tell me more about that."

Common Obstacles to Parts Dialogue

As you begin practicing parts dialogue, you might encounter some common challenges:

"I Don't Hear Anything" Some people expect parts dialogue to involve hearing clear, distinct voices. For many people, communication with parts is much more subtle - a sense of knowing what the part might say, a shift in body sensations, or an intuitive understanding of the part's perspective.

If you don't hear anything when you first reach out to a part, try:

- Asking more specific questions ("What are you most worried about?" rather than "How are you doing?")
- Paying attention to body sensations (tension, warmth, tightness) that might be the part's way of communicating

- Writing out your questions and seeing what comes through your hand onto paper
- Being patient - some parts take time to trust that this dialogue is safe

"It Doesn't Feel Real" Sometimes people worry they're just making up the dialogue or putting words in their parts' mouths. This is a normal concern that usually decreases with practice.

The test isn't whether the dialogue feels dramatically different from your normal thinking. The test is whether the conversation helps you understand yourself better and creates positive change in your internal system.

"My Part Won't Stop Talking" Some parts, especially those that have been ignored for a long time, might flood you with information once they have your attention. While this can feel overwhelming, it's usually a good sign - it means the part trusts you enough to share its experience.

If a part is overwhelming you with information, you can gently ask it to slow down: "I really want to hear everything you have to say, and I want to be able to take it all in. Could you help me by sharing one concern at a time?"

"My Part Is Being Hostile" Sometimes parts respond to initial dialogue attempts with anger, suspicion, or dismissiveness. This is often because the part has been criticized or ignored in the past and doesn't trust that this time will be different.

Don't take the hostility personally or get into an argument with the part. Instead, acknowledge the part's feelings: "I can see you don't trust me right now, and that makes sense. How can I show you that I genuinely want to understand your perspective?"

The Art of Parts Questions

Learning to ask good questions is one of the most important skills in parts dialogue. Good questions help parts feel seen and understood while giving you insight into their inner world.

Questions About Experience:
- What's it like to be you?
- How are you feeling right now?
- What's your biggest concern?
- What's been hardest for you lately?

Questions About History:
- When did you first start doing this job?
- What was happening in our life when you developed?
- What would have happened if you hadn't been there to help?
- Who taught you this strategy?

Questions About Fears:
- What are you most afraid will happen?
- What do you think would occur if you stopped doing your job?
- What threatens you the most?
- What keeps you up at night?

Questions About Needs:
- What do you need most right now?
- What would help you feel safer?
- How would you like to be treated?
- What would make your job easier?

Questions About Relationships:

- How do you get along with other parts of our system?
- Which parts do you work well with?
- Which parts do you conflict with?
- What would help you trust me more?

Marcus's First Dialogue

Marcus had been struggling with procrastination for months. Important projects would sit undone while he found endless distractions - cleaning the house, organizing his email, researching things he didn't need to know about. His typical response was to criticize himself for being lazy and irresponsible, which only made the procrastination worse.

After learning about parts dialogue, Marcus decided to try talking with his Procrastinator part instead of just fighting with it.

Marcus: "Procrastinator part, I've been getting really frustrated with you lately, but I realize I've never actually asked what's going on with you. What's it like when you take over and make me avoid important work?"

At first, Marcus didn't sense any response. But as he sat quietly, he became aware of a kind of tired, overwhelmed feeling.

Marcus: "Are you feeling overwhelmed by these projects?"

Suddenly Marcus had a clear sense of what his Procrastinator part might say: "These projects are too big and I don't know where to start. What if I mess them up? What if I'm not as competent as everyone thinks I am? It feels safer to not try than to try and fail."

Marcus: "So you're not actually lazy - you're scared. You're trying to protect me from failing by avoiding the possibility of failure altogether."

The relief Marcus felt at this realization told him he was on the right track. His Procrastinator wasn't sabotaging him - it was trying to protect him from potential shame and criticism.

Marcus: "What would help you feel more confident about tackling these projects?"

The response that came was immediate: "Break them into smaller pieces. Get some support or guidance instead of trying to figure everything out alone. And stop calling me lazy - I'm doing my best to help."

This single conversation shifted Marcus's entire relationship with his procrastination. Instead of fighting his Procrastinator part, he began working with it, creating detailed project plans and asking for help when he felt stuck.

Dialogue with Different Types of Parts

Different types of parts require slightly different approaches to dialogue:

Dialoguing with Critic Parts

Critic parts can be some of the most challenging to dialogue with because they're often so harsh and seemingly unreasonable. But underneath their harsh exterior, critic parts are usually trying to prevent shame, failure, or rejection.

Approach critic parts with:

- Acknowledgment of their hard work ("I can see you've been working really hard to help me improve")
- Curiosity about their fears ("What are you worried will happen if I'm not perfect?")
- Appreciation for their protective intention ("I understand you're trying to keep me safe from criticism")

Avoid:

- Arguing with their assessments ("That's not true!" or "You're being too harsh!")
- Trying to shut them down ("Just stop being so negative!")
- Taking their criticism at face value without understanding the underlying concern

Dialoguing with Anxious Parts

Anxious parts are often full of "what if" scenarios and catastrophic thinking. They're trying to prevent bad outcomes by thinking through every possible danger.

Approach anxious parts with:

- Validation of their concerns ("I can see why you'd be worried about that")
- Curiosity about specific fears ("What's the worst thing you imagine happening?")
- Appreciation for their vigilance ("Thank you for trying to keep us safe")

Avoid:

- Logical arguments about why their fears are unrealistic
- Dismissing their worries as "just anxiety"
- Trying to eliminate all uncertainty to make them feel better

Dialoguing with People-Pleasing Parts

People-pleasing parts are often focused on others' needs and reactions, sometimes to the exclusion of your own wellbeing. They're usually trying to ensure acceptance and avoid rejection or conflict.

Approach people-pleasing parts with:

- Recognition of their caring nature ("I can see how much you care about others")

- Curiosity about their fears ("What do you think will happen if someone gets upset with us?")
- Validation of their desire for connection ("I understand wanting to be liked and accepted")

Avoid:

- Criticizing them for being "too nice" or "weak"
- Demanding that they stop caring about others' reactions
- Forcing them to set boundaries before they feel safe doing so

Advanced Dialogue Techniques

As you become more comfortable with basic parts dialogue, you can experiment with more sophisticated approaches:

Parts Meetings Sometimes it's helpful to dialogue with multiple parts at once, especially when they're in conflict with each other. You can facilitate conversations between parts, helping them understand each other's perspectives and negotiate solutions.

Body-Based Dialogue Many parts communicate through physical sensations. You can ask parts to show you where they live in your body, what they feel like physically, or how they want to be touched or held.

Visual Dialogue Some people find it helpful to visualize their parts and dialogue with these images. You might see your Inner Critic as a stern teacher, your Anxious part as a worried child, or your Creative part as an artist. These visualizations can make dialogue feel more concrete and accessible.

Written Dialogue Writing out conversations with parts can be particularly effective for people who process better through written expression. You can write questions with your dominant hand and let parts respond through your non-dominant hand, or simply journal back and forth with different parts.

Sarah's Parts Meeting

Sarah had been feeling torn between her desire to advance her career and her wish to start a family. Her Ambitious part wanted to apply for a promotion that would require long hours and travel, while her Family-Oriented part wanted to focus on getting pregnant and creating a stable home life.

Instead of continuing to feel paralyzed by this internal conflict, Sarah decided to facilitate a conversation between these parts.

Sarah (to Ambitious part): "What's most important to you about getting this promotion?"

Ambitious part: "I've worked so hard to get to this point in my career. If I don't take this opportunity, I might never get another chance. I want to prove that I'm capable and successful."

Sarah (to Family-Oriented part): "And what's most important to you about starting a family now?"

Family-Oriented part: "I'm 32, and I don't want to wait too much longer. I want kids to be a priority, not something I squeeze in around a demanding career. I'm afraid if we wait for the 'perfect' time, it will never happen."

Sarah: "It sounds like you're both afraid of missing out on something important. Ambitious part, you're afraid of missing your career window, and Family-Oriented part, you're afraid of missing your family window."

Both parts agreed that this was accurate.

Sarah: "What if there were a way to honor both of your needs? What would that look like?"

Through continued dialogue, the parts developed a plan: Sarah would apply for the promotion but negotiate a modified schedule that would allow for family planning. If she got the job, she would work in the role for a year to prove herself, then discuss family-friendly policies with her employer. If she didn't get the promotion, she would focus on starting a family while continuing to build her skills for future opportunities.

Both parts felt heard and respected in this solution, and Sarah felt clear and confident about moving forward.

Your Parts Dialogue Practice This Week

This week, your primary focus is beginning to practice parts dialogue. Start with small, low-stakes conversations rather than trying to address your biggest internal conflicts immediately.

Choose One Part to Work With Select a part that's been active recently - maybe your Inner Critic, your People-Pleaser, or your Anxious part. Don't try to dialogue with multiple parts at first.

Set Aside Regular Time Even five to ten minutes a day can be enough to begin developing this skill. Consistency matters more than duration when you're starting out.

Stay Curious Approach your parts with genuine interest rather than an agenda to change them. The goal is understanding, not manipulation.

Be Patient Parts dialogue is a skill that develops over time. Don't worry if it feels awkward or artificial at first - that's completely normal.

Notice Changes Pay attention to shifts in your relationship with the part you're dialoguing with. Do you feel more compassionate toward it? Do you understand its perspective better? Do you feel less controlled or overwhelmed by it?

Building Internal Trust

The ultimate goal of parts dialogue isn't just communication - it's building trust within your internal system. When your parts feel genuinely heard and understood, they're more likely to collaborate with your Self-leadership rather than taking over unilaterally.

This trust develops gradually as parts experience being listened to without being judged, controlled, or dismissed. As trust grows, parts become more willing to share their deeper concerns, needs, and vulnerabilities.

Trust also grows as your Self proves to be a reliable leader - someone who can handle the information parts share, who takes their concerns seriously, and who works to find solutions that honor everyone's needs.

Moving Forward with Dialogue

Learning to talk with your parts opens up entirely new possibilities for self-understanding and internal harmony. Instead of being at the mercy of parts that seem to act independently, you become an active participant in your internal life.

This week's practice with basic parts dialogue prepares you for next week's work on negotiating with protector parts. Once you can communicate effectively with your parts, you can begin to work out agreements about when different parts' strategies are helpful and when they might step back to let other parts or your Self take the lead.

Parts dialogue is both simple and profound. Simple because it's just having conversations with aspects of yourself that are already active. Profound because it transforms your entire relationship with your internal world from conflict to collaboration.

Your parts have been waiting for you to listen to them with genuine curiosity and respect. They have wisdom to share, stories to tell, and important contributions to make to your life. The conversation starts now.

Chapter 10: Negotiating with Protectors

Your protector parts are like security guards for your internal system. They've been trained to watch for specific threats and respond with particular strategies. Some scan for signs of rejection and immediately activate people-pleasing protocols. Others monitor for potential failure and launch perfectionist countermeasures. Still others detect criticism and deploy defensive maneuvers.

The thing about security guards is that they're usually pretty good at their jobs. Your People-Pleaser has probably helped you avoid conflict and maintain relationships. Your Perfectionist has likely contributed to your success and achievements. Your Controller has probably prevented some chaos and problems in your life.

But security guards can also be overzealous. They might see threats where none exist, use outdated protocols for new situations, or restrict your freedom in the name of keeping you safe. When this happens, you need to **negotiate** with them - not fire them or override them, but update their job descriptions and help them work more skillfully.

Negotiating with protectors is different from general parts dialogue because protectors are specifically focused on keeping you safe. They often resist change because change feels dangerous. They're not being stubborn or difficult - they're being protective. Understanding this makes all the difference in how you approach them.

Why Protectors Resist Change

Before you can successfully negotiate with your protector parts, you need to understand why they often resist new ways of being, even when those new ways might be healthier or more effective.

They Have Historical Evidence Your protectors developed their strategies based on real experiences. Your People-Pleaser learned to avoid conflict because conflict felt dangerous in your family of origin. Your Perfectionist learned to avoid mistakes because mistakes led to criticism or rejection. These parts have evidence that their strategies work, even if that evidence is outdated.

They Don't Trust Self-Leadership Some protectors developed during periods when your Self-leadership wasn't available or effective. If you were overwhelmed, traumatized, or too young to handle certain situations, protectors stepped in to manage things. They might not trust that your Self can handle challenging situations now.

They See Their Jobs as Essential Protectors often believe that relaxing their vigilance, even slightly, will lead to disaster. Your Controller might think that if it stops trying to manage every detail, everything will fall apart. Your People-Pleaser might believe that if it stops monitoring others' moods, you'll be rejected and abandoned.

They're Afraid of Other Parts Many protectors are specifically trying to keep exile parts from being hurt again. Your tough, independent protector might be afraid that if it lets down its guard, your vulnerable parts will get hurt the way they did in childhood. Your achievement-oriented protector might be working overtime to prevent your "lazy" or "unreliable" parts from sabotaging your success.

The Negotiation Process

Negotiating with protectors is a collaborative process that respects their protective function while working toward more flexible and effective strategies. Here's how it typically works:

Step 1: Acknowledge Their Good Intentions

Start any negotiation by recognizing what your protector part is trying to do for you. This isn't just a therapeutic technique - it's acknowledging reality. Your protectors genuinely are trying to help, even when their methods are problematic.

You might say something like:

- "Inner Critic, I can see that you're trying to help me improve and avoid making mistakes."

- "People-Pleaser, I understand you're working hard to keep me liked and accepted."

- "Controller, I appreciate how you try to prevent chaos and keep things organized."

This acknowledgment is crucial because protectors that feel criticized or unappreciated are much more likely to dig in their heels and resist change.

Step 2: Understand Their Specific Concerns

Ask your protector what specifically it's afraid will happen if it changes its approach. The more specific you can get about their fears, the better you can address them.

Instead of general questions like "What are you worried about?" try:

- "What's the worst thing you imagine happening if I'm not perfect?"

- "If I stop trying to please everyone, what do you think will occur?"

- "If I let go of some control, what are you afraid might happen?"

Listen to these concerns without immediately trying to reassure or argue with them. Your protector's fears might seem irrational from your current adult perspective, but they made perfect sense when the protector developed.

Step 3: Validate Their Historical Experience

Help your protector know that you understand why it developed its strategies and acknowledge that these strategies were helpful at the time.

"I can see why you learned to be so careful about making mistakes - Dad's criticism was really harsh, and being perfect felt like the only way to avoid his anger."

"It makes total sense that you learned to watch everyone's moods so carefully - Mom's depression was scary, and keeping her happy felt like survival."

This validation isn't about agreeing that the old strategies are still necessary. It's about honoring your protector's intelligence and resourcefulness in developing solutions to real problems.

Step 4: Assess Current Reality Together

Once your protector feels heard and validated, you can begin exploring whether current circumstances require the same level of vigilance or the same specific strategies.

You might ask:

- "What's different about my life now compared to when you first developed this strategy?"
- "Are there any situations where your approach is still really needed?"
- "Are there contexts where it might be safe to try a different approach?"

This isn't about convincing your protector that its fears are unfounded. It's about collaboratively assessing whether the original strategies need updating for current circumstances.

Step 5: Negotiate New Agreements

Based on your understanding of your protector's concerns and your shared assessment of current reality, you can begin negotiating new ways of working together.

This might involve:

Updating job descriptions: "People-Pleaser, instead of trying to make everyone happy all the time, what if your job was to help me be considerate while still honoring my own needs?"

Agreeing on specific contexts: "Perfectionist, what if we use your high standards for work presentations but allow more flexibility for casual social media posts?"

Creating safety measures: "Controller, what if we try being more spontaneous on weekends, but keep your planning skills active for work projects?"

Establishing check-in times: "Inner Critic, instead of providing constant commentary, what if we scheduled regular times for you to share feedback and concerns?"

Julie's Negotiation with Her People-Pleaser

Julie had been struggling with her People-Pleaser part for years. This part made her say yes to every request, avoid any conversation that might cause conflict, and exhaust herself trying to keep everyone around her happy. Julie knew she needed boundaries, but every time she tried to set them, she felt overwhelming anxiety and guilt.

Instead of fighting her People-Pleaser, Julie decided to try negotiating with it.

Julie: "People-Pleaser, I know you work really hard to keep everyone happy, and I appreciate how much you care about my relationships. But I'm feeling really overwhelmed and resentful lately. Can we talk about this?"

People-Pleaser: "I have to keep everyone happy! If people get upset with you, they might leave. Remember what happened with Mom when you disappointed her? Remember how awful that felt?"

Julie: "I do remember that. Mom's silent treatment was really scary when I was eight. It made sense that you learned to avoid making anyone upset."

People-Pleaser: "Exactly! So I can't stop doing my job. It's too dangerous."

Julie: "I'm wondering, though - are all the people in my life now like Mom was? When my friend Sarah gets frustrated with me, does she give me the silent treatment for days?"

People-Pleaser: "Well... no. Sarah usually just tells me what's bothering her and then we work it out."

Julie: "And when my coworker Jake disagreed with my idea in the meeting, did he try to punish me or exclude me?"

People-Pleaser: "No, he was actually pretty respectful about it. And later he said he liked some aspects of my proposal."

Julie: "So it seems like not everyone reacts to disappointment or conflict the way Mom did. What if we could learn to tell the difference between people who can handle some disagreement and people who might react more extremely?"

Through continued dialogue, Julie and her People-Pleaser worked out a new agreement. The People-Pleaser would continue to help Julie be considerate and maintain good relationships, but it would allow Julie to express her genuine preferences with people who had proven themselves to be emotionally mature. They agreed to start with small experiments - expressing minor preferences with close friends - and gradually work up to bigger boundaries as the People-Pleaser gained confidence that Julie's relationships could handle some authenticity.

Common Negotiation Challenges

As you practice negotiating with your protectors, you'll likely encounter some predictable obstacles:

The All-or-Nothing Response Some protectors hear any suggestion for change as a demand to completely abandon their role. Your Perfectionist might interpret "you don't need to be perfect all the time" as "it's okay to be completely sloppy and careless."

When this happens, reassure your protector that you're not asking it to stop doing its job entirely. You're asking it to do its job more skillfully and efficiently.

The Slippery Slope Fear Protectors often worry that any relaxation of their vigilance will lead to complete chaos. "If I let you be imperfect on this small thing, pretty soon you'll be failing at everything."

Address this by proposing small experiments with built-in safety measures and regular check-ins. "What if we try being less perfectionist about answering emails, but keep your high standards for client presentations? We can see how it goes and adjust if needed."

The Trust Issue Some protectors simply don't trust that your Self can handle challenges without their constant intervention. This is especially common if the protector developed during a time when you were very young or overwhelmed.

Building this trust takes time and consistent demonstration. Start with low-stakes situations where you can show your protector that your Self is capable of handling difficulties skillfully.

The Loyalty Conflict Sometimes protectors resist change because they feel loyal to the people or circumstances that taught them their strategies. A protector that learned people-pleasing from an overwhelmed parent might feel like setting boundaries is betraying that parent's memory.

Acknowledge this loyalty while helping the protector understand that growing and changing can honor their origins: "We can appreciate what Mom taught us about caring for others while also learning to care for ourselves."

Advanced Negotiation Strategies

As you become more skilled at basic negotiation, you can try more sophisticated approaches:

Creating Parts Councils Sometimes multiple protectors need to be part of the negotiation process. If your People-Pleaser and your Boundary-Setter are in conflict, they both need to be part of finding a solution.

You can facilitate meetings between conflicting parts, helping them understand each other's concerns and find compromises that honor everyone's needs.

Updating Parts' Information

Sometimes protectors are operating with outdated information about your current life circumstances. Your Security-Seeking part might still think you're as financially vulnerable as you were in college, or your Social Anxiety part might not realize you've developed better social skills.

You can help protectors update their understanding by sharing information about your current resources, skills, and support systems.

Gradual Exposure Plans

For protectors that are very resistant to change, you can negotiate gradual exposure plans that allow them to test new approaches slowly and safely.

Your Controller might agree to let you be spontaneous for just one hour a week initially, with the understanding that if it goes well, you can gradually increase spontaneous time.

Creating Safety Signals

Some protectors need specific signs that it's safe to relax their vigilance. These might be external cues (being in certain environments or with certain people) or internal cues (feeling grounded in your body or connected to your Self-leadership).

Work with your protectors to identify what signals would help them know when their protective strategies are needed versus when they can step back.

David's Controller Negotiation

David's Controller part had been running his life since childhood, when his alcoholic father's unpredictable behavior made control feel like survival. As an adult, David's Controller helped him be successful at work, but it was also preventing him from enjoying life or being spontaneous with his family.

The Controller was particularly resistant to change because it had evidence of what happened when David wasn't vigilant - chaos, disappointment, and pain.

David: "Controller, I appreciate how hard you've worked to keep my life stable and predictable. You've helped me build a successful career and avoid a lot of problems."

Controller: "That's right. And if I stop managing everything carefully, it's all going to fall apart. You don't remember what it was like when Dad was drinking - the chaos, the unpredictability, the disappointment. I'm not going to let that happen again."

David: "I do remember some of that, and I understand why you developed such strong control strategies. They were exactly what I needed then. I'm wondering, though - what's different about my life now compared to when I was eight years old?"

Controller: "Well... you're not dependent on Dad anymore. You have your own job and house. You're married to someone stable. But still, things can go wrong. Life is unpredictable."

David: "That's true - life is unpredictable. What if instead of trying to control everything to prevent unpredictability, we focused your skills on helping me respond well to unpredictable things when they happen?"

This conversation led to a gradual negotiation process where David's Controller agreed to experiment with less control in low-stakes situations. They started with allowing David to go to restaurants without researching the menu beforehand, then progressed to taking family drives without predetermined destinations.

The Controller maintained its role in important areas - work projects, financial planning, family safety - while allowing David more spontaneity in areas where perfect control wasn't actually necessary.

Your Protector Negotiation Practice

This week, choose one protector part that's been particularly active or problematic in your life. Using the negotiation process outlined in this chapter, begin working toward a new agreement with this part.

Start Small Don't try to negotiate major changes immediately. Begin with small adjustments that feel manageable to both you and your protector.

Be Patient Negotiation with protectors often takes multiple conversations over weeks or months. Don't expect immediate transformation.

Honor Resistance If your protector is very resistant to change, spend more time in the validation and understanding phases before pushing for new agreements.

Test New Agreements Once you've negotiated a new approach, try it out in real-life situations. Pay attention to how your protector responds and be willing to adjust the agreement based on what you learn.

Maintain the Relationship Successful negotiation isn't a one-time event - it's an ongoing relationship. Check in regularly with your protectors about how the new agreements are working.

The Long-Term Benefits

When you successfully negotiate with your protector parts, the benefits extend far beyond just reducing problematic behaviors. You develop:

Internal Trust: Your protectors learn to trust your Self-leadership, making them less likely to take over reactively.

Flexibility: Instead of rigid, automatic responses, you develop the ability to choose strategies that fit current circumstances.

Self-Compassion: Understanding your protectors' good intentions makes it easier to be kind to yourself when you struggle.

Authentic Expression: As protectors feel more secure, they allow more of your authentic self to be expressed in relationships and activities.

Reduced Internal Conflict: When protectors feel heard and valued, they're less likely to fight with each other or with other parts of your system.

Building Collaborative Internal Leadership

Negotiating with protectors is ultimately about developing collaborative internal leadership. Instead of being dominated by protective strategies or fighting against them, you become a skilled coordinator who can work with all aspects of yourself.

This collaborative approach honors the wisdom and good intentions of your protective parts while also maintaining the flexibility and authenticity that come from Self-leadership. Your protectors become allies and advisors rather than dictators or obstacles.

Next week, you'll learn about safely approaching exile parts - the wounded, vulnerable aspects of yourself that your protectors work so hard to keep hidden and safe. This work requires even more delicacy and skill, but it's where some of the most profound healing happens in IFS work.

Your protectors have been faithful guardians of your internal system. They deserve to be treated with respect, appreciation, and skillful negotiation. When they feel truly heard and valued, they become some of your greatest resources for creating positive change.

Chapter 11: Safely Approaching Exiles

Working with exile parts is like approaching a wounded animal in the forest. These parts have been hurt, often repeatedly, and they've learned that people can be dangerous. They might hide when they sense someone approaching, or they might lash out in fear and pain. They need to know you're safe before they'll let you close enough to help.

Your exile parts carry your deepest wounds, your most authentic emotions, and often your greatest capacity for joy, creativity, and love. They're called exiles because they've been banished from everyday life by protector parts that believe keeping them hidden is the only way to prevent further hurt.

But exile parts don't want to stay hidden forever. They want to be seen, heard, understood, and integrated into your life. They have gifts to offer and healing to receive. The question isn't whether to work with your exiles - it's how to approach them in ways that feel safe for everyone involved.

This work requires more skill and patience than dialoguing with protectors because exile parts are more vulnerable and often more traumatized. They need extra reassurance that this time will be different from all the other times they were hurt, ignored, or abandoned.

Understanding Exile Vulnerability

Exile parts are vulnerable in ways that protector parts aren't. Protectors developed strategies and defenses; exiles got hurt before they could protect themselves. This fundamental difference shapes everything about how you approach them.

They Carry Young Energy Most exile parts feel much younger than your chronological age because they got stuck at the age when they were overwhelmed or traumatized. Your 35-year-old self might have an exile part that feels five years old and still experiences the world from that five-year-old perspective.

This young energy can be beautiful - it often carries wonder, spontaneity, and the capacity for pure joy. But it also means that exile parts can be easily overwhelmed by complexity, harshness, or adult-level responsibility.

They Remember Being Hurt Exile parts carry not just the memory of being hurt, but the felt sense that they're still in danger. Time doesn't heal exile parts the way it might heal other aspects of yourself. Your exile that was criticized harshly as a child still expects criticism. Your exile that was abandoned still fears abandonment.

This isn't because exile parts are irrational - from their perspective, they never got clear evidence that the world is different now. They've been locked away while your protectors handled the outside world, so they haven't had a chance to learn that you're now an adult with more resources and choices.

They Need Extra Safety Because of their vulnerability and history of being hurt, exile parts need much more reassurance about safety than protector parts do. A protector might be willing to negotiate after one or two conversations, but an exile might need many interactions before feeling safe enough to fully emerge.

This need for safety isn't neediness or weakness - it's intelligence. These parts learned that people can be dangerous, and they're not going to make themselves vulnerable again without substantial evidence that it's genuinely safe to do so.

Prerequisites for Exile Work

Before approaching exile parts directly, several conditions need to be in place:

Strong Self-Leadership

Working with exiles requires consistent access to your Self-qualities - curiosity, compassion, courage, and calmness. If you're frequently blended with protector parts or if your Self-leadership is shaky, exile work can be overwhelming or retraumatizing.

Spend time strengthening your capacity to stay present, grounded, and compassionate before approaching your most wounded parts. This isn't about being perfect - it's about having enough internal stability to hold space for vulnerable emotions and memories.

Protector Permission

Your protector parts developed specifically to keep your exiles safe. They will not let you near exile parts if they don't trust your intentions or your ability to handle what you find there.

This means you often need to work with protectors first, building their trust and getting their permission before approaching the exiles they protect. A protector might say something like, "I'll let you talk to that sad part, but I'm going to be right here watching, and if you hurt that part or get overwhelmed, I'm stepping in."

Adequate Support

Exile work can bring up intense emotions, difficult memories, and old pain that's been locked away for years or decades. Make sure you have adequate support systems in place - whether that's friends, family, a therapist, or other resources - before beginning intensive exile work.

This doesn't mean you need professional therapy to work with your exiles, but it does mean being realistic about your emotional capacity and having backup plans for times when the work feels overwhelming.

Realistic Expectations

Healing exile parts isn't a quick fix. These parts have been hurt for a long time, and they need time to learn that things can be different now.

Approach exile work with patience and long-term perspective rather than expecting immediate transformation.

The Process of Approaching Exiles

When you're ready to begin working with exile parts, the process typically follows these stages:

Stage 1: Getting Protector Permission

Start by checking in with the protector parts that guard your exiles. These might be Controller parts that keep you too busy to feel, Perfectionist parts that prevent you from being vulnerable, or Tough Guy parts that maintain emotional distance.

Ask these protectors:

- "Is it okay if I spend some time with the sad/scared/angry part you've been protecting?"
- "What do you need from me to feel comfortable with me approaching that exile part?"
- "What are you most worried will happen if I connect with that vulnerable part?"

Don't proceed until you have clear permission from protective parts. If they're resistant, spend more time understanding their concerns and building their trust in your Self-leadership.

Stage 2: Making Gentle Contact

Once you have protector permission, reach out to exile parts with extreme gentleness. Use the kind of voice you might use with a frightened child or injured animal - soft, reassuring, and non-threatening.

You might say something like:

- "Little one, I know you've been hurt, and I want you to know I'm here if you want to connect."

- "Sad part, I can sense that you're in there, and I want you to know that it's safe to let me know what's happening with you."
- "Sweet child, I know others have hurt you before, but I'm different. I want to understand your experience."

Don't be discouraged if there's no immediate response. Exile parts often need time to assess whether it's truly safe to emerge.

Stage 3: Listening Without Trying to Fix

When exile parts do begin to share their experience, the most important thing you can do is listen without immediately trying to fix, heal, or change anything. These parts need to be witnessed and understood before they can begin healing.

Listen for:

- What happened to this part
- How it felt at the time
- What it needed but didn't receive
- How it's been carrying these experiences
- What it most wants you to understand

Respond with validation and compassion:

- "That sounds so scary for you."
- "Of course you felt alone - no one was there to help you."
- "It makes sense that you're still afraid that could happen again."
- "I'm so sorry you had to go through that."

Stage 4: Offering What Was Needed

Once an exile part feels truly heard and understood, you can begin to offer what it needed during the original hurt but didn't receive. This might be:

Protection: "I won't let anyone hurt you like that again."

Comfort: "You don't have to be alone with this pain anymore."

Validation: "Your feelings make complete sense. You weren't being too sensitive or dramatic."

Love: "You are loveable exactly as you are. You don't have to earn love through being perfect or pleasing others."

Justice: "What happened to you was wrong. It wasn't your fault."

This offering needs to be genuine and specific to what the exile part actually needed. Don't just say what you think you should say - tune into what this particular part most longs to hear.

Stage 5: Bringing the Exile into Current Life

The ultimate goal of exile work is to help these parts know that they don't have to stay stuck in the past. They can come into your current life where they'll be protected by your adult Self and celebrated for their gifts.

This process, called "retrieval" in IFS, involves helping exile parts understand that:

- You're now an adult with more resources and choices
- You won't let them be hurt the way they were hurt before
- They have valuable contributions to make to your current life
- They don't have to carry their old burdens alone anymore

Maria's Work with Her Rejected Child

Maria had always struggled with feeling different and not belonging. She was successful professionally and had good friends, but she constantly felt like an outsider who was just pretending to fit in. This feeling was especially strong in group situations or when meeting new people.

As Maria explored her internal system, she discovered a young exile part that felt about seven years old and carried memories of being excluded and rejected by classmates in elementary school.

When Maria first approached this part, it was very frightened and suspicious.

Little Maria: "Are you going to hurt me too? Are you going to tell me I'm weird and that I don't belong?"

Adult Maria: "No, sweet one. I'm here because I care about you and I want to understand what happened to you."

Little Maria: "The kids at school said I was weird. They wouldn't let me sit with them at lunch. They laughed at my clothes and the way I talked. I tried to fit in but nothing worked."

Adult Maria: "That sounds so painful and lonely. No child should have to feel excluded like that."

Little Maria: "I just wanted someone to like me. I wanted to belong somewhere."

Adult Maria: "Of course you did. Every child needs to feel accepted and included. Those kids were mean to you, and that wasn't okay."

Through many conversations over several months, Adult Maria helped Little Maria understand that the rejection she experienced in second grade wasn't evidence that she was fundamentally unloveable or weird. It was evidence that some children can be cruel and that the school environment wasn't safe for her sensitive nature.

Adult Maria also helped Little Maria see that her current life was different. She had friends who appreciated her unique perspective, a career where her creativity was valued, and the skills to find people who were kind and accepting.

As Little Maria began to feel safer, she started contributing her natural enthusiasm and authenticity to Maria's social interactions. Instead of constantly trying to fit in, Maria found herself able to be more genuine, which actually made her more attractive to the kind of people she wanted to be friends with.

Common Challenges in Exile Work

Working with exile parts can bring up several predictable challenges:

Emotional Overwhelm

Exile parts often carry big emotions that have been suppressed for years. When they finally feel safe enough to express these feelings, it can feel overwhelming - both for the exile and for your system as a whole.

If you find yourself overwhelmed by an exile's emotions:

- Ask your protective parts to help you stay grounded
- Remind the exile that you're here now and they don't have to carry all the pain alone
- Take breaks if needed - you can always come back to continue the work
- Seek support from friends, family, or professionals if the emotions feel too big to handle

Protector Interference

Sometimes protector parts get nervous during exile work and try to shut it down. Your Controller might suddenly create a crisis that "requires" your immediate attention. Your Achiever might flood you with urgent tasks. Your Tough Guy might tell you that this work is "weak" or "self-indulgent."

When this happens:

- Acknowledge the protector's concerns: "I can see you're worried about this work."

- Reassure them about your intentions: "I'm doing this to help heal our whole system, not to make us more vulnerable."

- Negotiate timing: "What would help you feel more comfortable with me spending time with this exile part?"

Exile Flooding

Sometimes exile parts, once they feel safe, want to share everything all at once. They might flood you with memories, emotions, or needs that feel overwhelming.

If an exile is flooding you:

- Gently ask them to slow down: "I want to hear everything you have to share, and I need to be able to take it in. Could we go a little slower?"

- Set boundaries around timing: "I have about twenty minutes right now. Can we start with what's most important to share today?"

- Reassure them about your commitment: "I'm not going anywhere. We have time to work through all of this together."

Old Pain Resurfacing

Working with exiles can bring up old pain that feels fresh and immediate. You might find yourself crying about things that happened decades ago or feeling anger about old injustices with surprising intensity.

This is normal and healthy - exile parts need to feel their feelings fully in order to heal. But it can be disconcerting if you're not prepared for it.

When old pain resurfaces:

- Remember that feeling the pain is part of the healing process
- Offer comfort to the part that's hurting
- Don't try to rush the process or make the feelings go away quickly
- Seek support if the pain feels unmanageable

Advanced Exile Work Techniques

As you become more comfortable with basic exile work, you can experiment with more sophisticated approaches:

Inner Child Visualization

Some people find it helpful to visualize their exile parts as actual children and interact with them in imaginary settings. You might imagine taking your scared child to a safe place, playing with your creative child, or comforting your sad child.

Body-Based Healing

Many exile parts carry trauma in the body. You might work with these parts through gentle touch, movement, or breathing exercises that help them release stored tension and pain.

Creative Expression

Exile parts often respond well to creative forms of expression - drawing, writing, music, dance, or other artistic activities. These can provide ways for exiles to communicate that don't rely solely on words.

Reparenting Practices

Some exile work involves consciously providing the kind of parenting these parts needed but didn't receive. This might involve setting boundaries that protect your exiles, celebrating their achievements, or simply spending time with them in ways that feel nurturing and supportive.

Safety Guidelines for Exile Work

Because exile work can be intense and potentially destabilizing, it's important to follow some basic safety guidelines:

Go Slowly: Don't try to heal decades of wounding in a few weeks. Exile work is a long-term process that requires patience and persistence.

Maintain Support Systems: Make sure you have people you can talk to about your process, especially if difficult emotions or memories emerge.

Balance Exile Work with Other Life Activities: Don't spend all your time focused on internal work. Maintain your relationships, responsibilities, and activities that bring you joy.

Know When to Seek Professional Help: If exile work brings up trauma that feels unmanageable, suicidal thoughts, or symptoms that interfere with your daily functioning, seek professional support.

Trust Your Instincts: If something about the work doesn't feel right or safe, trust that instinct and slow down or seek guidance.

Your Exile Approach Practice

This week, begin the process of safely approaching one of your exile parts. Remember that this is just the beginning of a longer process, so don't expect dramatic results immediately.

Choose Your Exile Carefully: Start with an exile that feels accessible but not too overwhelming. Save the most wounded parts for when you have more experience and support.

Get Protector Permission: Make sure your protective parts are on board with this work before proceeding.

Move Slowly: Take your time building trust with your exile part. It's better to go too slowly than too quickly.

Practice Self-Compassion: This work can bring up difficult emotions. Be patient and kind with yourself as you navigate this process.

The Promise of Exile Healing

Working with exile parts is some of the most rewarding work you can do in your internal system. When exile parts feel safe, seen, and valued, they contribute incredible gifts to your life:

Authentic Emotion: Exile parts carry your capacity for genuine feeling - both painful and joyful emotions that haven't been filtered through protective strategies.

Creativity and Spontaneity: Many exile parts retain the natural creativity and playfulness that existed before life taught them to be careful and strategic.

Capacity for Intimacy: Exile parts often hold your ability to be genuinely vulnerable and connected with others.

Aliveness and Vitality: When exile parts feel safe to emerge, they bring energy and vitality that might have been missing from your life for years.

Wisdom and Intuition: Young parts often have access to intuitive wisdom that gets educated out of us as we learn to rely primarily on rational thinking.

Moving Toward Integration

Next week, you'll learn about the unburdening process - helping exile parts release the pain, beliefs, and roles they've been carrying so they can step into their natural gifts and contribute to your life in healthy ways.

Exile work requires courage, patience, and skill, but it's where some of the most profound healing happens. Your exile parts have been waiting for someone trustworthy to approach them with genuine care and compassion. That someone is you, operating from your Self-leadership with the support of your protective parts.

These parts of yourself have been in exile long enough. It's time to bring them home.

Chapter 12: The Unburdening Process

There's a moment in fairy tales when the spell breaks. The frog turns back into a prince, the beast becomes human again, or the cursed princess wakes from her endless sleep. Something that was trapped or transformed by difficult circumstances suddenly remembers its true nature and steps back into its authentic power.

The **unburdening process** in IFS work is similar to these fairy tale transformations. It's when exile parts release the pain, beliefs, and protective roles they've been carrying and remember who they really are underneath all the hurt.

Your exile parts didn't start out as wounded, fearful, or angry. They began as pure expressions of your authentic nature - curious, loving, creative, spontaneous, and alive. They only became burdened when life experiences taught them that these natural qualities were dangerous or unacceptable.

The unburdening process helps these parts release what doesn't belong to them so they can return to their essential nature. It's not about erasing their history or pretending their pain didn't happen. It's about helping them understand that they don't have to keep carrying that pain as their primary identity.

What Are Burdens?

In IFS language, **burdens** are the painful emotions, limiting beliefs, and protective roles that exile parts have taken on as a result of difficult experiences. These burdens are like heavy coats that your parts put on to survive harsh weather - they served a purpose at the time, but they're no longer needed and they're restricting movement.

Burdens might include:

Painful Emotions: Shame, terror, rage, despair, or loneliness that got stuck in your system when original experiences were too overwhelming to process completely.

Limiting Beliefs: "I'm not lovable," "The world is dangerous," "I can't trust anyone," "I'm worthless," or "I have to be perfect to be acceptable."

Protective Roles: Sometimes exile parts take on responsibilities that don't belong to them, like feeling responsible for their parents' happiness or believing they have to earn love through achievement.

Trauma Responses: Hypervigilance, dissociation, people-pleasing, or other survival strategies that made sense during traumatic situations but are no longer needed.

These burdens aren't part of your exile parts' true nature - they're add-ons that your parts picked up along the way. The goal of unburdening is to help these parts separate their essential selves from the pain they've been carrying.

The Natural Qualities of Unburdened Parts

When exile parts release their burdens, they typically return to natural qualities that are intrinsic to being human:

Joy and Playfulness: The capacity for spontaneous happiness, laughter, and fun that exists in healthy children.

Curiosity and Wonder: Natural fascination with the world and desire to learn and explore.

Love and Connection: The ability to give and receive love freely, without conditions or protective strategies.

Creativity and Expression: Artistic impulses, imagination, and the desire to create and contribute something unique to the world.

Authenticity: The ability to be genuinely yourself without performing or adapting to others' expectations.

Resilience: Natural ability to bounce back from difficulties and maintain hope about the future.

Wisdom and Intuition: Access to inner knowing that goes beyond rational analysis.

These qualities don't need to be developed or learned - they need to be uncovered. They're already present in your exile parts, waiting to emerge once the burdens are released.

When Unburdening Is Appropriate

Unburdening is advanced IFS work that should only be attempted when certain conditions are met:

Strong Therapeutic Relationship: If you're working with a therapist, you need to have established trust and safety in that relationship. If you're doing self-work, you need to have developed a solid relationship with your own Self-leadership.

Exile Trust: The exile part needs to trust you enough to be vulnerable about its deepest pain and fears. This usually requires multiple sessions of building relationship before unburdening is possible.

Protector Permission: Your protector parts need to be on board with the unburdening process. If they're worried that letting the exile release its burdens will make it vulnerable to being hurt again, they'll interfere with the process.

Adequate Support: Unburdening can bring up intense emotions and memories. Make sure you have adequate support systems in place to handle whatever emerges.

Stable Life Circumstances: While you don't need perfect life circumstances to do this work, avoid attempting unburdening during major life crises or when you're under extreme stress.

The Unburdening Process

When the conditions are right, the unburdening process typically follows these stages:

Stage 1: Identifying the Burdens

Work with your exile part to identify what specific burdens it's been carrying. This requires careful listening because exile parts might not initially distinguish between their essential nature and the pain they've taken on.

Ask questions like:

- "What feelings have you been carrying since that difficult time?"
- "What did you learn about yourself or the world that felt heavy or painful?"
- "What role did you take on that wasn't really yours to carry?"
- "What beliefs about yourself formed during that experience?"

Listen without judgment as your exile describes what it's been carrying. Often these parts have been holding onto burdens for so long that they think the burdens are just "who they are."

Stage 2: Recognizing the Burdens Aren't Theirs

Help your exile part understand that these burdens don't belong to them - they're things the part took on in response to difficult circumstances.

You might say something like:

- "That shame you've been carrying - that came from how others treated you, not from who you really are."
- "The belief that you can't trust anyone - that was a reasonable response to being betrayed, but it's not the truth about all relationships."
- "The fear you carry - that made sense when you were in danger, but you don't have to keep carrying it now that you're safe."

This stage often involves helping the exile part distinguish between what happened to them and who they are at their core.

Stage 3: Asking if They're Ready to Release

Once the exile understands that its burdens are add-ons rather than essential parts of its identity, ask if it's ready to let them go.

Some parts are immediately ready to release their burdens. Others need more time, reassurance, or support. Don't rush this process - let the exile part decide when it feels safe to let go.

You might ask:

- "Are you ready to let go of this shame that's been weighing you down?"

- "Would you like to release this fear now that you know you're safe?"

- "What would it be like to put down this heavy responsibility you've been carrying?"

Stage 4: The Release Process

If the exile is ready to release its burdens, there are several ways this can happen:

Energetic Release: Many parts experience unburdening as energy leaving their body. They might feel lighter, more spacious, or like something heavy has been lifted off them.

Symbolic Release: Some parts prefer to imagine releasing burdens in symbolic ways - throwing them into a fire, washing them away in a river, or handing them over to a higher power.

Emotional Release: The unburdening might involve crying, shaking, or other forms of emotional expression as old energy moves out of the system.

Verbal Release: Some parts want to speak their burdens out loud, declaring their intention to let go of what no longer serves them.

Physical Release: The unburdening might involve movement, breathing exercises, or other physical activities that help energy shift in the body.

The specific form of release isn't as important as the exile part's experience of genuinely letting go of what it's been carrying.

Stage 5: Welcoming the Natural Self

Once the burdens are released, invite the exile's natural qualities to emerge. This might involve:

Asking what's there now: "Now that you've released that burden, what are you aware of in yourself?"

Welcoming natural qualities: "I can see your joy/creativity/love emerging. Welcome back."

Celebrating the transformation: "You seem so much lighter and more yourself now."

Asking about gifts: "What gifts do you have to offer now that you're not weighed down by those old burdens?"

This stage is often accompanied by a noticeable shift in the exile's energy - from heavy and painful to light and vibrant.

Stage 6: Integration

The final stage involves helping the unburdened exile find appropriate ways to contribute to your current life. This might include:

Identifying where this part's gifts are needed: "Your creativity would be really valuable in that project you're working on."

Creating space for the part's expression: "How can we make sure your playful nature gets to show up regularly?"

Establishing ongoing relationship: "How can I stay connected with you so you don't have to carry burdens again?"

Rebecca's Unburdening Journey

Rebecca had been working with a Sad Child exile for several months. This part carried the pain of being emotionally neglected during Rebecca's parents' messy divorce when she was eight years old. The Sad Child felt responsible for her parents' unhappiness and had taken on the burden of trying to fix everyone else's emotions ever since.

After many sessions of building trust and understanding, Rebecca and her Sad Child were ready to attempt unburdening.

Rebecca: "Sweet one, you've been carrying so much responsibility for other people's feelings since Mom and Dad got divorced. You believed that if you could just make everyone happy, maybe they would stay together."

Sad Child: "I tried so hard, but nothing I did worked. I thought it was my fault that they were sad and angry all the time."

Rebecca: "What you took on - thinking you were responsible for their emotions - that was way too big a job for an eight-year-old. That responsibility never belonged to you."

Sad Child: "But if I don't take care of everyone's feelings, who will? What if people get hurt?"

Rebecca: "Adults are responsible for managing their own emotions. You were just a little kid who needed taking care of, not someone who should have been taking care of the adults."

Sad Child: "I've been carrying this for so long. I don't know who I am without it."

Rebecca: "Would you like to find out? Are you ready to let go of this responsibility that was never yours?"

Sad Child: "I'm scared, but yes. I'm tired of carrying this."

Rebecca guided her Sad Child through a visualization where the part imagined taking off a heavy backpack filled with everyone else's emotions and handing it over to Rebecca's adult Self to handle appropriately.

As the Sad Child released this burden, she experienced a profound shift. The heavy, responsible energy lifted, and underneath was a joyful, creative, spontaneous part that loved to sing, dance, and make art. This natural child energy had been buried under decades of inappropriate responsibility.

Over the following weeks, Rebecca found herself feeling lighter, more playful, and more creative than she had in years. She started taking art classes, being more spontaneous with friends, and setting better boundaries around other people's emotional needs.

Signs of Successful Unburdening

When unburdening is successful, you'll typically notice several changes:

The Exile Feels Lighter: The part reports feeling less weighed down, more spacious, or more like its true self.

Natural Qualities Emerge: Joy, creativity, love, or other essential qualities become more accessible and prominent.

Reduced Reactivity: The exile is less likely to get triggered by situations that previously caused intense reactions.

Increased Integration: The exile's gifts and qualities become more naturally available in daily life.

Better Relationships: As burdens are released, relationships often improve because you're relating from your authentic self rather than from wounded patterns.

Physical Changes: Many people report feeling physically different after unburdening - more energy, less tension, improved health.

Emotional Freedom: Emotions feel more fluid and appropriate to current situations rather than being stuck in old patterns.

When Unburdening Doesn't Work

Sometimes the unburdening process doesn't proceed smoothly. This might happen because:

Insufficient Trust: The exile doesn't yet trust enough to be vulnerable about its deepest burdens.

Protector Interference: Protective parts are worried about the exile becoming vulnerable and interfere with the process.

Incomplete Processing: The exile still needs more time to share its story and feel understood before it's ready to release burdens.

External Stressors: Current life circumstances are too stressful or chaotic to support the vulnerability required for unburdening.

Need for Professional Support: Some burdens, especially those related to significant trauma, may require professional therapeutic support to release safely.

If unburdening doesn't work the first time, that doesn't mean it will never work. It just means more preparation is needed - more trust-building, more protector work, or more support.

Maintaining Unburdened States

Once an exile has successfully unburdened, it's important to maintain the new state and prevent the part from taking on new burdens:

Regular Check-ins: Stay in relationship with your unburdened parts to make sure they're continuing to feel free and expressed.

Protective Boundaries: Your Self and protector parts need to maintain boundaries that prevent exile parts from being overwhelmed or traumatized again.

Appropriate Expression: Create regular opportunities for your unburdened parts' natural qualities to be expressed in your daily life.

Continued Support: Maintain the support systems that made unburdening possible in the first place.

Your Unburdening Readiness Assessment

Before attempting unburdening work this week, honestly assess whether you're ready:

Do you have a strong, trusting relationship with at least one exile part? Are your protector parts generally supportive of deeper healing work? Do you have adequate support systems for intense emotional work? Are your current life circumstances relatively stable? Do you have experience staying in Self-leadership during difficult emotions?

If you answered yes to most of these questions, you might be ready to begin exploring unburdening with one of your exile parts. If not, continue with basic relationship-building and consider seeking additional support.

The Ripple Effects of Unburdening

When exile parts release their burdens and return to their natural states, the effects ripple throughout your entire system and life:

Other Parts Relax: When exiles feel genuinely safe and free, protector parts can relax their vigilance and develop more flexible strategies.

Self-Leadership Strengthens: As internal conflict decreases, it becomes easier to maintain Self-leadership in challenging situations.

Relationships Improve: When you're relating from unburdened, authentic parts rather than wounded patterns, relationships become more genuine and satisfying.

Creativity Increases: Unburdened exile parts often carry tremendous creative energy that becomes available for new projects and expressions.

Physical Health Improves: Releasing emotional burdens often leads to improvements in physical symptoms and overall vitality.

Life Direction Clarifies: As authentic desires and values emerge from unburdened parts, your life direction often becomes clearer and more aligned with your true nature.

The Ongoing Journey

Unburdening isn't a one-time event - it's an ongoing process of helping your parts release what doesn't belong to them and step into their authentic nature. Some parts may need multiple unburdening sessions, while others transform dramatically in a single session.

The work continues as you support your unburdened parts in expressing their gifts, protect them from taking on new burdens, and help other parts in your system go through their own healing journeys.

This week, if you feel ready, begin exploring the possibility of unburdening work with one of your exile parts. If you're not ready yet, continue building relationships and trust with your parts while working toward the conditions that make unburdening safe and effective.

The goal isn't to rush toward unburdening, but to move at the pace that feels right for your system. Your exile parts have waited this long to be free - they can wait a little longer to make sure the process happens safely and effectively.

When exile parts truly unburden and return to their essential nature, they bring gifts that can transform not only your internal world but also your relationships, your work, and your contribution to the world. These parts have been in exile long enough. It's time for them to come home to themselves.

Completing the Dialogue and Healing Phase

You've now moved through the core healing work of IFS - learning to dialogue with your parts, negotiate with your protectors, safely approach your exiles, and begin the unburdening process. This represents a fundamental shift from being unconsciously driven by your parts to consciously collaborating with them.

The dialogue skills you've developed create the foundation for all ongoing IFS work. When you can communicate directly with your parts, you're no longer guessing about what's happening inside you or feeling helpless when parts take over. You have tools for understanding, negotiating, and coordinating your internal system.

Working with protectors through negotiation rather than force creates sustainable change. Your protective parts become allies rather than obstacles when they feel heard, valued, and appropriately involved in decision-making. This collaborative approach honors the wisdom of your protective strategies while updating them for current circumstances.

The exile work - approaching wounded parts with safety and care - opens pathways to authentic emotion, creativity, and aliveness that may have been locked away for years or decades. When exile parts feel genuinely safe and valued, they contribute tremendous vitality and authenticity to your life.

The unburdening process, when appropriate and safely conducted, can create profound transformation as parts release pain that never belonged to them and return to their essential nature. This work often produces lasting changes that ripple through every aspect of your life.

As you move into the final phase of this eight-week journey, you'll focus on integration - taking everything you've learned about your internal system and applying it to daily life decisions, relationships, and ongoing self-leadership. The goal is making IFS a practical, sustainable approach to living rather than just an interesting psychological framework.

The healing work you've done in these two weeks creates the foundation for lifelong internal collaboration. Your parts now know they can trust you to listen, understand, and work with them skillfully. This trust makes all future internal work more effective and sustainable.

Next week, you'll learn how to apply your IFS skills to practical decision-making, relationship challenges, and maintaining Self-leadership in the complexity of daily life. The journey from understanding to integration begins now.

Section IV: Integration and Daily Life (Weeks 7-8)

Chapter 13: Parts-Aware Decision Making

Every decision you make is a negotiation between your parts. Should you take that job offer? Your Security-Seeking part says yes because of the salary, while your Values-Driven part says no because the company culture feels wrong. Should you end that relationship? Your Loyal part wants to keep trying, but your Self-Respect part knows you deserve better treatment.

Most people make decisions by either letting the loudest part win or trying to ignore their parts entirely and be "rational." But there's a third option: **parts-aware decision making**. This approach involves consciously including all relevant parts in the decision process, understanding what each part needs and fears, and finding solutions that honor your whole system.

Parts-aware decision making doesn't mean every part gets to vote on everything. Your Worried part doesn't need a say in what to have for lunch, and your Perfectionist part doesn't need to be involved in casual weekend plans. But for important decisions - career changes, relationship choices, major purchases, life transitions - consulting your parts can lead to choices that feel more authentic, sustainable, and genuinely satisfying.

When you make decisions without consulting your parts, you often end up with internal sabotage, regret, or a sense that something important is missing from your choice. But when you include your parts skillfully in the decision process, you tap into the wisdom of your whole system and create choices that all aspects of yourself can support.

The Traditional Decision-Making Trap

Most decision-making advice focuses on logical analysis - making pros and cons lists, researching options, or using rational frameworks to evaluate choices. This approach has value, but it misses a crucial element: the emotional and intuitive intelligence of your parts.

Your Cautious part might have important information about risks that your logical mind hasn't considered. Your Creative part might see possibilities that don't show up on a spreadsheet. Your gut instinct about a person or situation might be your Intuitive part picking up on subtle cues that your rational mind missed.

When you try to make decisions purely rationally, several problems emerge:

Parts go underground but don't disappear. Your People-Pleaser might agree to a job that sounds good on paper, but if your Independence-Loving part hates the micromanaging culture, you'll find yourself feeling resentful and looking for ways to escape.

You miss important information. Parts carry emotional and somatic intelligence that complements logical analysis. Your Anxious part's concerns might actually be intuitive awareness of real problems that your optimistic thinking is overlooking.

Decisions feel hollow. When parts aren't included in decision making, the final choice might be technically correct but feel emotionally unsatisfying. You get what you thought you wanted but find it doesn't bring the fulfillment you expected.

Self-sabotage increases. Parts that weren't consulted about a decision often sabotage its implementation. Your Health-Conscious part might choose a gym membership, but if your Comfort-Seeking part wasn't included in the decision, you'll find reasons to skip workouts.

The Parts-Aware Decision Process

Parts-aware decision making is a structured approach that includes your parts as valuable advisors while maintaining Self-leadership over the final choice. Here's how it works:

Step 1: Identify the Decision and Get Centered

Clearly define the decision you need to make and create space for a thoughtful process. This isn't the approach to use for small, everyday choices, but it's invaluable for significant decisions that will impact your life direction.

Take some time to get centered in your Self-leadership. You can't facilitate an effective parts consultation if you're blended with anxiety, pressure, or any other part that might interfere with clear thinking.

Step 2: Invite Parts Input

Ask your internal system what parts have opinions, concerns, or input about this decision. You might say something like, "I'm considering taking this new job. Which parts of me have thoughts or feelings about this choice?"

Listen for the different voices that emerge. Don't evaluate their input yet - just collect information about who cares about this decision and why.

Common parts that show up in decision making include:

Security-Focused Parts: Parts concerned with safety, financial stability, or risk management

Values-Driven Parts: Parts that care about meaning, purpose, and alignment with your principles

Relationship Parts: Parts focused on how decisions will affect your connections with others

Growth Parts: Parts interested in learning, challenge, and personal development

Comfort Parts: Parts that prioritize ease, familiarity, and avoiding stress

Creative Parts: Parts that want opportunities for expression and innovation

Step 3: Interview Each Part Separately

Once you've identified which parts have input about the decision, interview each one individually. This prevents parts from arguing with each other and ensures you understand each perspective fully.

Ask each part questions like:

- What's most important to you about this decision?
- What are you hoping will happen if we make this choice?
- What are you afraid might happen?
- What would you need to feel good about whatever we decide?
- What information do you have that might be helpful?

Really listen to each part's perspective without immediately evaluating whether it's "right" or "reasonable." Parts often have wisdom that isn't immediately apparent.

Step 4: Look for Creative Solutions

With input from all relevant parts, look for solutions that honor as many concerns as possible. This often requires creative thinking that goes beyond the original options you were considering.

Maybe your Security part wants financial stability and your Adventure part wants travel. Instead of choosing between a stable office job and a risky travel career, you might find freelance work that allows both financial security and location independence.

Perhaps your People-Pleaser wants to maintain a friendship and your Boundary-Setter knows the person is draining your energy. Instead of choosing between continuing the friendship and ending it abruptly, you might gradually reduce contact while being kind when you do interact.

Step 5: Test Internal Consensus

Once you've identified a potential solution, check with your parts about how it feels. You're not looking for unanimous enthusiasm -

that's rarely possible. But you are looking for general agreement that the solution is workable and honors everyone's core needs.

Ask questions like:

- How does this solution feel to each of you?
- What concerns do you still have?
- What would need to be added or changed to make this work better?
- Can you support this decision even if it's not your first choice?

Step 6: Make the Decision from Self

With input from your parts and a solution that honors your whole system, make the final decision from your Self-leadership. This means the choice comes from your core values, wisdom, and long-term perspective rather than from any single part's agenda.

Sometimes this means choosing an option that isn't any single part's first preference but works for the system as a whole. Other times it means going with one part's strong preference while finding ways to address other parts' concerns.

Step 7: Create Implementation Support

Once you've made the decision, work with your parts to create support for implementing it successfully. This might involve:

Addressing lingering concerns: If your Cautious part is still worried about risks, create backup plans or safety measures.

Celebrating the choice: Let parts that are excited about the decision express their enthusiasm.

Managing resistance: If some parts are disappointed, acknowledge their feelings and find ways to honor their needs in other areas of life.

Creating accountability: Ask parts that care about the decision's success to help with follow-through.

Michael's Career Decision

Michael had been offered a promotion at his current company and was also considering a job offer from a startup. On paper, the promotion seemed like the obvious choice - more money, more security, clear advancement path. But something didn't feel right about it.

Instead of analyzing the decision purely logically, Michael decided to try a parts-aware approach.

Michael's parts consultation revealed:

Security Part: "The promotion is clearly better - more money, better benefits, less risk. The startup could fail and then where would we be?"

Growth Part: "The startup offers way more learning opportunities. At the current company, I'll just be doing more of the same work. I'm getting bored and need new challenges."

Creative Part: "The startup is working on really innovative products. I'd get to use my design skills in ways that aren't possible in our current corporate environment."

People-Pleasing Part: "My boss expects me to take the promotion. He's been grooming me for this role. If I turn it down, he'll be really disappointed."

Independence Part: "I hate the bureaucracy and politics at the current company. The startup would give me more autonomy and direct impact."

Status Part: "The promotion comes with a fancy title that would look great on my resume. The startup role is more junior-sounding."

Initially, Michael felt paralyzed by these conflicting perspectives. But as he listened more carefully, he realized that most parts shared some common values - they all wanted him to grow, contribute meaningfully, and have financial stability.

Michael got creative and went back to the startup with a counter-offer that addressed his Security part's concerns - he negotiated for equity, a higher starting salary, and a clear path to senior-level responsibility. He also had honest conversations with his current boss about his need for growth and innovation.

The creative solution that emerged was taking the startup job with better financial terms while maintaining a positive relationship with his current company by offering to do some consulting work during the transition.

All of Michael's parts felt heard in this solution. His Security part was satisfied with the improved financial package. His Growth and Creative parts were excited about the new challenges. His People-Pleasing part felt good about handling the transition respectfully. His Independence part was thrilled about the autonomy. And his Status part was satisfied that the consulting arrangement maintained his reputation in the industry.

Common Decision-Making Scenarios

Let's look at how parts-aware decision making applies to some common life situations:

Relationship Decisions

Relationship choices often involve complex negotiations between parts:

Your Attachment part wants closeness and connection **Your Independence part** values freedom and autonomy **Your Security part** seeks stability and predictability **Your Growth part** wants challenge and development **Your People-Pleasing part** tries to avoid conflict **Your Authentic part** wants to be genuinely yourself

In healthy relationship decisions, you find partners and relationship structures that honor multiple parts rather than requiring you to sacrifice important aspects of yourself.

Career Transitions

Career decisions typically involve:

Your Achiever part wanting success and advancement **Your Security part** needing financial stability **Your Creative part** seeking meaningful and engaging work **Your Social part** caring about workplace relationships **Your Values part** requiring alignment with your principles **Your Work-Life Balance part** protecting your personal time

Good career decisions find ways to honor multiple parts rather than forcing trade-offs between all your needs.

Major Purchases

Significant purchases often involve:

Your Practical part focusing on utility and value **Your Pleasure part** wanting beauty and enjoyment **Your Security part** worrying about financial impact **Your Status part** caring about image and perception **Your Environmental part** considering sustainability **Your Future-Planning part** thinking about long-term needs

Health and Lifestyle Choices

Health decisions frequently involve:

Your Health-Conscious part prioritizing physical wellbeing **Your Comfort part** wanting ease and familiar routines **Your Social part** considering how changes affect relationships **Your Perfectionist part** wanting to do everything "right" **Your Realistic part** knowing what's actually sustainable

When Parts Can't Agree

Sometimes even thorough parts consultation doesn't lead to consensus. When parts remain in significant disagreement, you have several options:

Compromise Solutions

Look for middle-ground approaches that give each part something they want, even if no part gets everything.

Sequential Solutions

Let different parts have their preferences at different times. Your Adventure part gets to choose this year's vacation while your Security part gets to focus on building savings.

Experimental Approaches

Try one approach for a limited time with agreement to reassess. Your parts might agree to test a new living situation for six months before making a permanent decision.

Values-Based Tiebreaking

When parts truly can't agree, make the decision based on your core values and long-term vision for your life. Some decisions require Self-leadership to choose a direction that serves your overall growth and wellbeing.

Time-Sensitive Decisions

Parts-aware decision making works best when you have time for thoughtful consultation. But what about decisions that need to be made quickly?

Even in urgent situations, you can do abbreviated parts check-ins:

Quick body scan: Notice what physical sensations arise with different options. Your parts often communicate through felt sense.

Gut reaction: Pay attention to your immediate response to each option. This is often parts communicating quickly.

Values alignment: Ask which option best aligns with your core values and long-term vision.

Regret test: Imagine yourself a year from now looking back on each choice. Which would you be more likely to regret?

Sarah's Moving Decision

Sarah had been living in New York for eight years when she was offered a great job in Portland. She had three weeks to decide, which felt like a lot of pressure but was enough time for thoughtful parts consultation.

Her parts had strong opinions:

Adventure Part: "Portland sounds amazing - great food scene, outdoor activities, completely different culture. This could be exactly the change we need."

Security Part: "New York is expensive, but at least we know how to navigate here. We have friends, we know the city, we have professional connections. Starting over is risky."

Career Part: "The Portland job is a big step up in responsibility and would open new professional opportunities. But New York has more options if this job doesn't work out."

Social Part: "I love our friend group here. It took years to build these relationships. What if we can't make friends in Portland? What if we get lonely?"

Financial Part: "The cost of living in Portland is so much lower. We could actually save money and maybe even buy a house eventually."

Family Part: "Moving would mean being farther from Mom and Dad. They're getting older and might need help soon."

Sarah realized that her parts were essentially debating between security and growth. After several internal conversations, she came up with a creative solution: she would take the Portland job for two years with a plan to reassess then. If Portland worked out, she'd stay. If not, she'd use the experience and savings to return to New York in a stronger position.

This timeline satisfied her Adventure and Career parts while giving her Security and Social parts confidence that the move wasn't permanent unless it was genuinely working well.

Building Your Decision-Making Skills

Parts-aware decision making is a skill that improves with practice. Start by using this approach for medium-sized decisions where you can afford to take time and experiment with the process.

Practice with lower-stakes choices: Try consulting your parts about weekend plans, restaurant choices, or small purchases to get comfortable with the process.

Notice your default patterns: Pay attention to which parts usually dominate your decision making and which ones rarely get heard.

Experiment with different approaches: Some people prefer written dialogue with their parts, others like internal conversation, and others find movement or visualization helpful.

Trust the process: Parts-aware decision making often leads to creative solutions that wouldn't have emerged from purely rational analysis.

Your Decision-Making Practice This Week

This week, choose one significant decision you're facing and work through it using the parts-aware process outlined in this chapter.

Set aside adequate time: Don't rush this process. Good parts consultation takes time and reflection.

Stay curious: Approach your parts' input with genuine interest rather than immediately judging which perspectives are "right."

Look for creative solutions: Don't assume you have to choose between your parts' different preferences. Often there are solutions that honor multiple perspectives.

Trust your Self-leadership: While parts input is valuable, the final decision should come from your Self, considering your long-term vision and core values.

The Long-Term Benefits

When you consistently make decisions with parts awareness, several benefits emerge:

Better follow-through: When parts feel included in decisions, they're more likely to support implementation rather than sabotage it.

Reduced regret: Decisions that honor your whole system are less likely to leave you feeling like something important was overlooked.

Increased self-trust: As you get better at consulting your parts and making decisions that work for your whole system, you develop more confidence in your decision-making abilities.

More authentic choices: Parts-aware decisions tend to be more aligned with who you really are rather than who you think you should be.

Better outcomes: When you include emotional and intuitive intelligence alongside rational analysis, you often make choices that work better in practice.

Parts-aware decision making transforms choice from internal warfare into internal collaboration. Instead of fighting with yourself about what to do, you become a skilled facilitator who can help all aspects of yourself work together toward solutions that serve your whole life.

Your parts have wisdom to offer about every significant choice you face. The question isn't whether to listen to them - they're already influencing your decisions whether you're aware of it or not. The question is whether you'll learn to include them consciously and skillfully in the process.

Chapter 14: Relationships Through an IFS Lens

Every relationship you have is actually a relationship between multiple internal systems. When you're talking to your partner, it's not just "you" talking to "them" - it's your parts interacting with their parts, creating a complex dance of protection, connection, triggering, and healing.

Your People-Pleaser part might be responding to their Critic part. Your Independent part might be reacting to their Controller part. Your Wounded Child part might be getting activated by their Distant part, while their Anxious part is being triggered by your Avoidant part.

Understanding relationships through an **IFS lens** changes everything. Instead of thinking "My partner is being controlling" or "I'm too needy," you start to see "My partner's Controller part is active right now" and "My Needy part is getting triggered." This shift from identity to parts creates space for curiosity, compassion, and more skillful responses.

When you understand the parts dynamics in your relationships, you can respond to others' parts from your Self-leadership rather than reacting from your own activated parts. You can also take responsibility for your own parts' contributions to relationship dynamics without losing yourself in shame or defensiveness.

How Parts Show Up in Relationships

Your parts don't disappear when you're with other people - in fact, they often become more active. Relationships are inherently triggering because they activate our deepest needs for connection, safety, and acceptance while also bringing up our fears of rejection, abandonment, and judgment.

Parts That Seek Connection

The People-Pleaser works overtime in relationships, trying to keep others happy and comfortable. This part monitors others' moods and adjusts its behavior accordingly, often sacrificing authenticity for harmony.

The Caretaker focuses on others' needs and problems, finding value and identity in being helpful. This part might neglect its own needs while being highly attuned to what others require.

The Entertainer tries to keep relationships light and fun, using humor, charm, or performance to maintain connection and avoid deeper or more difficult conversations.

The Lover seeks romantic and intimate connection, sometimes becoming focused on chemistry and passion to the exclusion of practical compatibility.

Parts That Protect from Hurt

The Defender argues, justifies, or attacks when it feels criticized or misunderstood. This part believes that the best defense is a good offense and may escalate conflicts to avoid feeling vulnerable.

The Withdrawer pulls away emotionally or physically when relationships feel too intense or risky. This part protects by creating distance and limiting vulnerability.

The Controller tries to manage others' behavior to feel safe in the relationship. This part might give unsolicited advice, make plans unilaterally, or try to change their partner.

The Tester creates drama or conflict to see if the other person will stay. This part believes that love isn't real unless it survives challenges and rejection.

Parts That Carry Wounds

The Rejected Child expects to be abandoned or excluded and may either cling desperately or push others away preemptively.

The Criticized Child feels shame easily and may become defensive, perfectionistic, or withdrawn when it perceives any negative feedback.

The Invisible Child feels unseen and unimportant, may become clingy or attention-seeking, or alternatively may hide its needs to avoid further disappointment.

The Betrayed Part has difficulty trusting others and may test loyalty constantly or remain emotionally guarded even in close relationships.

Julia's Relationship Pattern

Julia had a pattern in romantic relationships that confused and frustrated her. She would start relationships feeling confident and independent, but gradually become more anxious and clingy as the relationship developed. Partners would initially be attracted to her self-sufficiency but eventually feel overwhelmed by her neediness.

When Julia learned about parts, she began to understand this pattern differently.

At the beginning of relationships, Julia's **Independent part** was in charge. This part had learned to be self-sufficient after Julia's parents' messy divorce when she was twelve. The Independent part was genuinely attractive - it was confident, interesting, and didn't need constant reassurance.

But as relationships became more serious, Julia's **Abandoned Child** would get activated. This part carried the fear and pain from when her father left and rarely contacted her again. The Abandoned Child was terrified of being left again and would start monitoring her partner's behavior for signs of withdrawal.

When the Abandoned Child took over, Julia would:

- Text frequently and get anxious if her partner didn't respond quickly
- Ask for constant reassurance about the relationship

- Get upset when her partner wanted to spend time with friends
- Read rejection into normal relationship fluctuations

Partners would feel the shift from Julia's confident independence to anxious neediness, and many would indeed start to pull away, which confirmed the Abandoned Child's fears about relationships.

Once Julia understood this pattern as parts dynamics rather than character flaws, she could start working with it differently. She learned to:

Recognize when her Abandoned Child was getting triggered instead of being taken over by the feelings

Communicate about her needs from her Self rather than from the desperate energy of the activated part

Reassure her Abandoned Child that adult Julia had more resources and choices than twelve-year-old Julia did

Stay connected to her Independent part's wisdom even when her vulnerable parts were active

This awareness transformed Julia's relationships. Instead of swinging between extremes, she could maintain her essential independence while also being appropriately vulnerable about her needs and fears.

Understanding Others' Parts

Learning to recognize parts in other people is just as important as understanding your own parts. When you can see that someone's behavior is coming from a part rather than their whole Self, you can respond more skillfully and with more compassion.

Common Relationship Parts in Others

The Critic in others might show up as constant complaints, pointing out flaws, or having high standards that feel impossible to meet. This part is usually trying to prevent disappointment or maintain control.

The Wounded Child in others might appear as emotional reactivity, neediness, or sensitivity to perceived slights. This part is usually seeking the love and attention it didn't get earlier in life.

The Controller in others might manifest as micromanaging, giving unsolicited advice, or trying to make decisions for you. This part is typically trying to prevent chaos or unpredictability.

The People-Pleaser in others might show up as inability to express preferences, excessive agreeableness, or resentment that builds up over time. This part is usually avoiding conflict or rejection.

Responding to Others' Parts from Self

When you recognize that someone else's part is active, you have choices about how to respond:

Don't Take It Personally

When someone's Critic part is active and they're being judgmental, that behavior is coming from their protective strategy, not from accurate assessment of your worth. When someone's Wounded Child is being reactive, their emotional intensity is about their historical pain, not necessarily about your current behavior.

This doesn't mean you should accept bad treatment, but it does mean you don't have to absorb others' parts-driven behavior as truth about yourself.

Respond to the Part, Not Just the Behavior

Instead of just reacting to what someone is doing, try to understand what part might be driving the behavior and what that part needs.

If your partner's Controller part is being micromanaging, instead of just getting defensive, you might say, "I can see you're feeling worried about how this is going to turn out. What would help you feel more secure about this?"

If a friend's People-Pleaser is being overly accommodating, you might check in: "I want to make sure we're doing something you actually want to do. What would you prefer?"

Set Boundaries with Parts, Not People

Sometimes you need to set boundaries with specific parts rather than with the whole person. You might say something like:

"I love you and I'm not willing to be talked to that way when your Angry part is activated. Can we take a break and talk about this when you're feeling calmer?"

"I care about you and I notice your Worried part is trying to manage my decisions. I need you to trust that I can handle this myself."

Support Others' Self-Leadership

One of the most helpful things you can do in relationships is to support others in accessing their Self-leadership rather than enabling their parts to stay blended.

Instead of trying to calm someone's Anxious part by providing constant reassurance, you might help them connect with their own inner resources: "You seem really worried about this. What do you know in your wise self about how to handle this situation?"

Instead of trying to manage someone's Angry part by walking on eggshells, you might maintain your own Self-leadership and invite them to do the same: "I can see you're really upset. I want to understand what's happening for you, and I need us to talk about this respectfully."

Parts Dynamics in Relationship Conflicts

Most relationship conflicts involve parts getting triggered and reacting to each other. Understanding these dynamics can help you interrupt destructive patterns and find more productive ways to work through disagreements.

The Criticism-Defense Cycle

This common pattern happens when one person's Critic part activates the other person's Defender part, which then triggers the first person's Critic even more strongly.

Partner A's Critic: "You never help with the dishes. I'm tired of being the only one who cares about keeping the house clean."

Partner B's Defender: "That's not true! I helped yesterday, and I've been working really hard this week. You're being unfair."

Partner A's Critic: "See? You can't even take responsibility. You always make excuses instead of just helping."

Once you recognize this as a parts interaction, you can interrupt it:

Partner B from Self: "I can hear that you're frustrated about the dishes. Your concerns are valid, and I want to work this out. I'm feeling defensive right now, so can we take a short break and come back to this when we're both feeling calmer?"

The Pursuit-Distance Cycle

This pattern involves one person's Connection-Seeking part chasing the other person's Independence or Overwhelmed part, which creates more distance, which activates more pursuit.

Partner A's Connection-Seeker: "We never talk anymore. I feel like we're roommates, not partners."

Partner B's Overwhelmed part: "I need some space to decompress after work. I can't handle heavy conversations every day."

Partner A's Connection-Seeker: "You're always too tired or too busy. When are we supposed to connect?"

Partner B's Overwhelmed part: (Withdraws further)

Breaking this cycle requires both partners to understand their parts and take responsibility for them:

Partner A from Self: "I notice my part that needs connection is feeling anxious about us, and I don't want to pressure you. What would work better for both of us in terms of staying connected?"

Partner B from Self: "I can see your need for connection is important, and I also need some transition time after work. What if we planned some focused time together after I've had thirty minutes to decompress?"

Navigating Triggered States

When parts get triggered in relationships, the key is to recognize what's happening and respond from Self-leadership rather than reacting from your own triggered parts.

When Your Parts Get Triggered

Pause: Instead of immediately reacting, take a moment to recognize that a part is activated.

Identify the part: "My Rejected Child is feeling hurt right now" or "My Controller is getting anxious about this conflict."

Self-soothe: Connect with your Self-leadership and offer comfort to the triggered part.

Communicate from Self: When you're calmer, share your experience without blaming your partner for your parts' reactions.

Example: "When you seemed distant during dinner, my part that worries about connection got really scared that you were mad at me. I know that's my stuff, and I'm curious about what was actually going on for you."

When Your Partner's Parts Get Triggered

Stay in Self: Don't let your parts get activated by their parts. This is challenging but crucial for breaking reactive cycles.

Show curiosity: Instead of defending or attacking, get curious about what's happening for them.

Validate the part: Acknowledge their part's experience without necessarily agreeing with their interpretation.

Invite Self-leadership: Support them in connecting with their own Self rather than staying blended with the triggered part.

Example: "I can see something I said really upset you. I care about you and want to understand what happened. Can you help me understand what you heard and what part of you got hurt?"

Creating Parts-Aware Relationships

The most fulfilling relationships happen when both people understand parts dynamics and support each other's Self-leadership. This creates safety for all parts while maintaining authentic connection between whole people.

Characteristics of Parts-Aware Relationships

Parts get acknowledged without taking over: Both people can recognize when parts are active without letting those parts drive the whole relationship.

Self-to-Self connection is prioritized: The core relationship is between each person's Self, with parts being valued aspects of each person rather than the primary drivers.

Triggers are opportunities for healing: When parts get activated, it's seen as information and opportunity for growth rather than evidence of relationship problems.

Boundaries protect everyone's parts: Both people take responsibility for managing their own parts while being considerate of their partner's parts.

Communication includes parts awareness: People can say things like "My anxious part is worried about this" or "I notice your protective part is active right now."

Maria and David's Relationship Transformation

Maria and David had been married for twelve years, but their relationship had become increasingly conflicted and distant. David worked long hours and seemed emotionally unavailable, while Maria felt lonely and resentful. Their conversations often devolved into criticism and defensiveness.

When they learned about IFS, they began to understand their dynamic differently.

David's parts pattern: His Achiever part worked long hours to prove his worth and provide for the family. When he came home, his Overwhelmed part just wanted quiet and space. His Emotionally Distant part had learned in childhood that feelings were dangerous and best avoided.

Maria's parts pattern: Her Connection-Seeking part felt starved for intimacy and attention. Her Lonely Child carried pain from feeling unseen, which made her feel desperate for David's attention. Her Critic part would attack David for being unavailable, which made his Distant part withdraw even more.

Instead of continuing to see each other as the problem, they began to see how their parts were interacting in ways that triggered each other.

David learned to:

- Recognize when his Achiever was working compulsively and negotiate work boundaries
- Communicate to Maria when his Overwhelmed part needed space instead of just withdrawing
- Challenge his Distant part's belief that emotions were dangerous

Maria learned to:

- Soothe her Lonely Child instead of expecting David to fix her loneliness

- Express her need for connection from her Self rather than from her desperate parts
- Understand that David's withdrawal wasn't about her worth

Over time, they developed new patterns:

- David would let Maria know when he needed decompression time and when he'd be available for connection
- Maria would spend time with friends and hobbies to meet some of her social needs instead of relying entirely on David
- They scheduled regular connection time that honored both David's need for predictability and Maria's need for intimacy
- When parts got triggered, they could recognize it and take responsibility for their own internal work

Their relationship transformed from a battle between triggered parts to a collaboration between two people committed to understanding and supporting each other's whole internal systems.

Your Relationship Practice This Week

This week, choose one important relationship in your life and begin applying IFS awareness to your interactions.

Notice your parts in relationships: Pay attention to which of your parts are most active with different people and in different relationship contexts.

Practice recognizing others' parts: Instead of taking others' behavior personally, try to see what parts might be driving their actions.

Experiment with Self-to-Self communication: When conflicts arise, try to respond from your Self-leadership rather than from triggered parts.

Support others' Self-leadership: Look for opportunities to invite the people in your life to connect with their own Self-leadership rather than staying blended with reactive parts.

Growing Together

The most beautiful aspect of parts-aware relationships is how they create space for everyone to grow. When your parts feel seen and accepted by others, they can relax their protective strategies. When you understand and have compassion for others' parts, you can love them more completely.

Parts-aware relationships aren't about being perfect or never getting triggered. They're about creating conscious, compassionate partnerships that support everyone's journey toward wholeness and authenticity.

Next week, you'll learn about maintaining Self-leadership in the midst of life's ongoing challenges and complexities. The goal isn't to eliminate parts activation, but to develop the skills to return to Self-leadership consistently and quickly when parts take over.

Your relationships are some of your greatest opportunities for healing and growth. When you bring parts awareness to your connections with others, you transform not only your own internal world but also the quality of love and understanding you can offer to the people who matter most to you.

Chapter 15: Maintaining Self-Leadership

You're in the middle of a stressful workday when your boss sends an email questioning your latest project. Within seconds, your Inner Critic is attacking you for making mistakes, your Defensive part is crafting justifications, and your People-Pleaser is panicking about disappointing everyone. Your Self-leadership - that calm, wise center you've been cultivating - feels completely inaccessible.

Or you're having a conversation with your teenage daughter when she rolls her eyes and says something disrespectful. Your Authoritarian part wants to lay down the law immediately, while your Wounded Parent part feels hurt and rejected. The Self-led response you'd planned - staying calm and setting boundaries with love - disappears under the flood of activated parts.

This is the challenge of **maintaining Self-leadership** in real life. It's one thing to access your Self when you're sitting quietly doing internal work. It's quite another to stay Self-led when parts are getting triggered by the daily stresses, conflicts, and pressures of actual living.

The goal isn't to never have parts get activated - that's impossible and wouldn't even be healthy. The goal is to develop the ability to recognize when parts have taken over and return to Self-leadership quickly and effectively. It's about building what we might call "Self-leadership resilience" - the capacity to bend without breaking and return to your center even when life gets chaotic.

Understanding Self-Leadership Under Pressure

Self-leadership isn't a constant state - it's a dynamic process of coordination and rebalancing. Even people with strong Self-leadership have moments when parts take over. The difference is how quickly they recognize what's happened and how skillfully they return to Self-led functioning.

Research in neuroscience shows that under stress, our brains naturally prioritize reactive, survival-oriented responses over thoughtful, integrated ones (Van der Kolk, 2014). This means that maintaining Self-leadership requires conscious practice and specific skills, especially during challenging times.

Factors That Challenge Self-Leadership

Several factors can make it more difficult to maintain Self-leadership:

Stress and overwhelm: When your system is overloaded, parts often take over to manage specific aspects of the situation. Your Controller might try to handle logistics while your Emotional part gets flooded.

Fatigue: When you're tired, you have less capacity for the conscious awareness and emotional regulation that Self-leadership requires.

Triggers from the past: When current situations resemble past hurts or traumas, exile parts can get activated suddenly and intensely, overwhelming your capacity for Self-leadership.

Multiple demands: When you're trying to manage competing priorities - work deadlines, family needs, health issues - different parts might take over different areas, fragmenting your sense of integration.

Relationship conflicts: Interpersonal triggers can activate parts very quickly, especially in relationships where you have strong attachment or investment.

Major life changes: Transitions like job changes, relationship shifts, or health challenges can activate multiple parts simultaneously as your system tries to adapt.

The Self-Leadership Recovery Process

When you notice that parts have taken over, you can use a systematic process to return to Self-leadership:

Step 1: Recognize the Takeover

The first step is simply noticing that you're not in Self-leadership anymore. This awareness often comes through physical sensations, emotional intensity, or recognizing familiar patterns.

Signs that parts have taken over include:

- Feeling emotionally hijacked or out of control
- Physical tension or activation (tight jaw, clenched fists, racing heart)
- Thinking in black-and-white terms
- Losing access to curiosity or compassion
- Reacting automatically without conscious choice
- Feeling like "this isn't really me"

Step 2: Pause and Ground

Instead of continuing to react from parts, create a pause. This might be as simple as taking three deep breaths, as structured as excusing yourself for a bathroom break, or as intentional as asking for time to think before responding.

Grounding techniques that can help:

- Feel your feet on the floor
- Notice your breath without trying to change it
- Look around and name five things you can see
- Gently stretch or move your body
- Touch something with an interesting texture

Step 3: Ask Parts to Step Back

Once you've created a bit of space, gently ask the activated parts to give you room to access your Self-leadership. You might say internally:

"I can see you're really activated right now, and I want to understand what's happening. Can you give me a little space so I can think clearly about this situation?"

"Thank you for trying to protect me. I need to handle this from a calmer place. Can you let me take the lead here?"

Step 4: Access Self-Qualities

Intentionally connect with Self-qualities like curiosity, compassion, calmness, or courage. You might ask yourself:

"What would be most helpful in this situation?" "If I were at my wisest and most centered, how would I respond?" "What does my heart know about what's needed here?"

Step 5: Respond from Self

Once you've accessed some Self-leadership, respond to the situation from that more centered place. Your response might be very different from what the activated parts wanted to do.

Step 6: Follow Up with Parts

After handling the immediate situation, check in with the parts that were activated to understand what triggered them and what they need to feel more secure going forward.

Jennifer's Self-Leadership Recovery

Jennifer was in a team meeting when her colleague Mark interrupted her presentation to point out what he thought was an error in her analysis. Jennifer's Shame part immediately flooded her with embarrassment, while her Defensive part wanted to argue with Mark publicly.

Recognition: Jennifer felt her face get hot and noticed the familiar surge of shame and anger that meant her parts were taking over.

Pause and Ground: Instead of immediately responding, Jennifer took a slow breath and felt her feet on the floor.

Ask Parts to Step Back: Internally, she said, "I know you're upset about being interrupted and challenged. Let me handle this professionally, and we can talk about it later."

Access Self-Qualities: Jennifer connected with her professional competence and genuine curiosity about Mark's concern.

Respond from Self: "Thanks for bringing that up, Mark. Let me look at that section again. You might be right about that calculation."

Follow Up with Parts: After the meeting, Jennifer acknowledged her Shame part's hurt at being publicly questioned and her Defensive part's anger at Mark's interruption. She was able to soothe both parts while also recognizing that Mark's feedback was actually helpful.

This whole process took less than thirty seconds, but it transformed what could have been a defensive argument into a professional collaboration.

Daily Practices for Self-Leadership Maintenance

Rather than just recovering Self-leadership when it's lost, you can build practices that help maintain it more consistently:

Morning Self-Connection

Start each day with a brief internal check-in. Ask yourself:

- How am I feeling today?
- What parts might need attention?
- What does my Self know about what's most important today?
- What would support my Self-leadership throughout the day?

This doesn't need to be a long meditation - even two or three minutes of conscious self-connection can set a different tone for your whole day.

Regular Self-Leadership Breaks

Throughout the day, take brief moments to reconnect with your Self-leadership. This might happen:

- Between meetings or major tasks
- Before difficult conversations
- When you notice stress building up
- During transitions (driving, walking, etc.)

These mini-breaks help prevent parts from building up so much activation that they take over completely.

End-of-Day Integration

Before sleeping, spend a few minutes reviewing your day from Self-leadership:

- What went well today?
- When did parts take over, and what can I learn from that?
- What parts need appreciation for their efforts today?
- What does my Self know about tomorrow's priorities?

This practice helps you learn from your experiences and start the next day from a more integrated place.

Physical Self-Care

Your capacity for Self-leadership is directly connected to your physical wellbeing. Parts are more likely to take over when you're hungry, tired, or physically stressed.

Self-leadership supportive practices include:

- Regular sleep on a consistent schedule
- Nutritious meals eaten at regular intervals
- Some form of physical movement or exercise
- Time in nature when possible
- Activities that help you feel grounded in your body

Relationship Practices

Since relationships are major triggers for parts activation, developing relationship skills supports Self-leadership:

Communicate your internal experience: "I notice I'm getting triggered by this conversation. Can we slow down?"

Take responsibility for your parts: "My defensive part is getting activated. That's not about you - I just need a moment to center myself."

Support others' Self-leadership: "You seem really stressed. What would help you feel more grounded right now?"

Creating Self-Leadership-Friendly Environments

You can also modify your environment to support Self-leadership maintenance:

At Work

- Take regular breaks instead of pushing through fatigue
- Set boundaries around availability and workload when possible
- Communicate proactively about challenges instead of waiting until you're overwhelmed
- Create physical spaces that feel calming (plants, photos, comfortable lighting)

At Home
- Establish routines that support your parts (transition time after work, regular meals, predictable bedtimes)
- Minimize unnecessary stressors where possible
- Create physical spaces for Self-connection (meditation corner, comfortable reading chair)
- Communicate with family members about your needs and theirs

In Relationships
- Practice speaking from Self rather than from activated parts
- Ask for what you need instead of expecting others to anticipate your needs
- Set boundaries that protect your capacity for Self-leadership
- Spend time with people who support your Self-leadership rather than constantly trigger your parts

Working with Chronic Self-Leadership Challenges

Some people face ongoing challenges that make Self-leadership particularly difficult to maintain:

Trauma History

People with significant trauma history might have parts that are chronically activated or Self-leadership that developed later in life. This doesn't mean Self-leadership is impossible, but it might require:

- Professional support to help stabilize parts that are easily triggered
- Extra attention to safety and grounding practices
- Patience with the process of developing Self-leadership capacity

- Recognition that healing happens over time

High-Stress Life Circumstances

Some life circumstances - caring for sick family members, financial crises, major life transitions - create ongoing stress that challenges Self-leadership. In these situations:

- Focus on maintaining Self-leadership for short periods rather than constantly
- Ask for help and support from others when possible
- Lower expectations for yourself while maintaining core practices
- Remember that this is a temporary situation that will eventually change

Mental Health Challenges

Depression, anxiety, ADHD, and other mental health conditions can make Self-leadership more difficult. This doesn't mean IFS isn't helpful, but it might mean:

- Combining IFS work with appropriate medical or therapeutic treatment
- Recognizing that some days will be harder than others
- Celebrating small victories in maintaining Self-leadership
- Being patient and compassionate with yourself during difficult periods

Marcus's Self-Leadership Journey

Marcus struggled with maintaining Self-leadership during his daily commute. Traffic would trigger his Impatient part, which would get angry at other drivers, and his Stressed part, which would start worrying about being late and all the work waiting at the office.

Marcus decided to treat his commute as Self-leadership practice time:

Before starting the car: Marcus would take a moment to connect with his intention to stay Self-led during the drive.

During the drive: When he noticed parts getting activated by traffic, he would:

- Take a deep breath
- Ask his parts to relax
- Listen to calming music or podcasts
- Practice gratitude for things he could see
- Remind himself that arriving a few minutes late wasn't actually dangerous

After arriving: Marcus would sit in his car for a minute and appreciate his efforts to stay Self-led, even when it was challenging.

Over time, Marcus found that his commute became less stressful and he arrived at work in a much better state of mind. He also discovered that the Self-leadership skills he practiced during driving helped him in other areas of life.

Advanced Self-Leadership Practices

As you become more skilled at basic Self-leadership maintenance, you can experiment with more advanced practices:

Parts Meetings

Regularly scheduled internal meetings where you check in with your various parts, understand their current concerns, and negotiate how they'll work together in the coming period.

Seasonal Self-Leadership Planning

Adjusting your Self-leadership practices based on predictable stressors (busy work seasons, holidays, anniversary dates of difficult events).

Self-Leadership in Service

Using your Self-leadership not just for personal benefit but to contribute positively to your family, workplace, and community. When you're consistently Self-led, you become a calming, stabilizing presence for others.

Crisis Self-Leadership Protocols

Developing specific plans for how you'll maintain Self-leadership during predictable crises (work emergencies, family conflicts, health scares).

Your Self-Leadership Maintenance Practice

This week, focus on developing sustainable practices for maintaining Self-leadership in your daily life:

Choose one daily practice: Pick a morning check-in, regular breaks, or evening integration practice that feels manageable and sustainable.

Identify your common triggers: Notice what situations, people, or circumstances most frequently activate your parts.

Practice the recovery process: When you notice parts taking over, experiment with the six-step process for returning to Self-leadership.

Create environmental supports: Make one change to your work, home, or relationship environment that supports your Self-leadership.

The Ongoing Journey

Maintaining Self-leadership is a lifelong practice, not a destination you reach. There will always be new challenges that test your capacity to stay centered, and there will always be opportunities to deepen your Self-leadership skills.

The goal isn't perfection - it's progress. Each time you recognize that parts have taken over and consciously return to Self-leadership, you're strengthening your capacity for this kind of conscious living. Each time you respond to a trigger from Self rather than from a reactive part, you're contributing to your own healing and the healing of your relationships.

Self-leadership under pressure is one of the greatest gifts you can give yourself and others. When you can stay centered in the midst of chaos, curious in the face of conflict, and compassionate when everyone around you is reactive, you become a source of stability and healing in the world.

Your Self-leadership matters - not just for your own wellbeing, but for everyone whose life you touch. This is the heart of IFS work: helping people access their innate capacity for wisdom, compassion, and skillful action, even in the most challenging circumstances.

Chapter 16: Your Ongoing IFS Practice

Eight weeks ago, you began a journey into your internal world. You discovered that you're not a single, consistent self but rather a complex system of parts, each with their own history, wisdom, and contributions to make. You learned to recognize when different parts are active, understand what they're trying to accomplish, and work with them as allies rather than obstacles.

But this book ending doesn't mean your IFS journey is complete. In many ways, you're just getting started. The concepts and skills you've learned over these eight weeks are foundations for a lifelong practice of conscious, compassionate self-leadership.

IFS as a way of life means bringing parts awareness to every aspect of your experience - your relationships, your work, your creative expression, your response to challenges and opportunities. It means treating yourself with the same curiosity and respect you'd show a good friend, even when your parts are struggling or making mistakes.

The question isn't whether you'll continue to have parts conflicts, triggers, or moments when you lose Self-leadership. You will. The question is how quickly you'll recognize what's happening and how skillfully you'll work with your internal system to return to balance and wisdom.

The Lifelong Nature of IFS Work

Parts work isn't therapy you complete and then move on from. It's more like learning a language - once you understand the basics, you can keep developing fluency and nuance throughout your life. There's always more to discover about your internal system, new parts to meet, deeper relationships to develop, and more sophisticated ways to coordinate your internal family.

Your parts will continue to change as you encounter new life circumstances. Becoming a parent might activate nurturing parts you didn't know you had. Career changes might require parts that have been dormant to step forward. Loss and grief might awaken parts that carry deep wisdom about love and impermanence.

The beauty of IFS as a lifelong practice is that it grows with you. The same frameworks that help you understand simple internal conflicts can also support you through major life transitions, relationship challenges, creative projects, and spiritual growth.

Building Your Personal IFS Practice

Just as everyone's internal system is unique, everyone's IFS practice will be different. Some people are drawn to daily meditation and journaling with their parts. Others prefer to use IFS skills as needed when conflicts or challenges arise. Some integrate parts awareness into their creative work, while others focus primarily on relationship applications.

The key is finding approaches that work for your life, personality, and circumstances. Here are some elements to consider as you build your ongoing practice:

Daily Connection Practices

Morning check-ins: Starting your day with a brief internal conversation can help you understand what parts might need attention and what your Self knows about the day's priorities.

Evening integration: Ending your day by reviewing what parts were active, what worked well, and what you learned helps consolidate insights and prepare for better Self-leadership tomorrow.

Transition moments: Using the spaces between activities - walking to your car, waiting in line, sitting down to eat - as opportunities to briefly connect with your internal state.

Body awareness: Since parts often communicate through physical sensations, developing sensitivity to your body's signals helps you recognize parts activation more quickly.

Weekly and Monthly Practices

Parts journaling: Regular writing about your internal experience helps you track patterns, notice changes, and deepen relationships with your parts.

Parts meetings: Scheduled internal conversations where you check in with various parts about current life circumstances and upcoming challenges.

Self-leadership review: Regularly assessing how well you're maintaining Self-leadership and what supports or challenges your capacity for conscious coordination.

Integration planning: Thinking ahead about how to apply IFS insights to upcoming situations, relationships, or decisions.

Seasonal and Annual Practices

Life transition support: Using IFS frameworks to navigate major changes like job transitions, relationship shifts, or life stage developments.

Anniversary awareness: Recognizing that certain times of year might activate particular parts due to historical associations and planning extra support during these periods.

Goal setting from wholeness: Making decisions about life direction by consulting your whole internal system rather than just your ambitious or security-focused parts.

Healing retreats: Periodically taking time for deeper internal work, whether through professional support, personal retreats, or intensive self-exploration.

Sarah's Five-Year IFS Journey

Sarah first learned about IFS during a period of career burnout and relationship struggles. Her initial practice focused on basic parts recognition - learning to identify when her People-Pleaser was taking over at work and when her Critic was attacking her after social interactions.

Over the first year, Sarah developed a morning practice of checking in with her internal system and an evening practice of appreciating her parts' efforts during the day. She learned to recognize her common triggers and developed skills for returning to Self-leadership when parts took over.

By the second year, Sarah was using IFS frameworks for major life decisions. When she was considering whether to move to a new city, she consulted with her Adventure part (excited about new experiences), her Security part (worried about leaving her job and friends), her Growth part (interested in new challenges), and her Comfort part (attached to familiar routines). The decision she made honored multiple parts' needs and felt genuinely sustainable.

In years three and four, Sarah's practice deepened to include relationship applications. She learned to recognize when her partner's parts were triggered and respond from Self-leadership rather than from her own reactive parts. She also began supporting friends and family members in understanding their own parts patterns.

By year five, Sarah described IFS as "just how I think about being human." She naturally included parts awareness in her parenting, her work as a teacher, her creative writing, and her community involvement. Parts work had become less like a practice she did and more like a lens through which she understood herself and others.

Common Challenges in Long-Term Practice

As you develop your ongoing IFS practice, you might encounter some predictable challenges:

Practice Inconsistency

Like any skill, IFS work benefits from regular practice. But life gets busy, crises arise, and it's easy to fall out of connection with your internal world.

When this happens:

- Start small rather than trying to resume a complex practice all at once
- Use difficult situations as reminders to reconnect with IFS skills
- Be patient with yourself rather than self-critical about inconsistency
- Remember that even brief moments of parts awareness are valuable

Spiritual or Psychological Bypassing

Sometimes people use IFS concepts to avoid dealing with practical problems or difficult emotions. "That's just my anxious part" can become a way of dismissing legitimate concerns rather than understanding and addressing them.

Healthy IFS practice involves:

- Taking parts' concerns seriously even when you don't act on them immediately
- Using Self-leadership to address practical problems rather than just understanding them
- Recognizing that some situations require action, not just internal work
- Balancing parts understanding with appropriate responsibility and accountability

Over-Pathologizing Normal Emotions

Learning about parts can sometimes lead to seeing pathology everywhere. Normal sadness becomes "my depressed part," regular frustration becomes "my angry part taking over," and ordinary life stress becomes evidence of internal dysfunction.

Remember that:

- Having parts is normal and healthy
- Strong emotions aren't necessarily evidence that parts have taken over
- Some situations genuinely warrant intense emotional responses
- The goal is conscious coordination, not emotional flatness

Relationship Challenges

As you develop IFS awareness, you might become frustrated with people who don't understand parts concepts or who seem to be "living from their parts" all the time.

Healthy relationship approaches include:

- Using IFS to understand others without trying to diagnose or fix them
- Focusing on your own Self-leadership rather than trying to manage others' parts
- Sharing IFS concepts only when others are genuinely interested
- Remembering that people have different paths to growth and healing

Avoiding Professional Help When Needed

IFS is a powerful self-help framework, but it's not a substitute for professional support when that's needed. Some situations require therapy, medical intervention, or other specialized help.

Consider professional support when:

- You're dealing with significant trauma that feels overwhelming to approach alone
- Parts work brings up suicidal thoughts or seriously self-destructive impulses
- You have mental health conditions that benefit from professional treatment
- Relationship or family problems require outside mediation or support
- You want to deepen your IFS work with someone trained in advanced techniques

Advanced IFS Applications

As your practice matures, you might explore more sophisticated applications of IFS principles:

Creative Expression

Many people find that understanding their parts enhances their creative work. Your Critic part might step back to let your Creative part play. Your Perfectionist might learn to collaborate with your Experimental part rather than shutting it down.

Professional Life

IFS awareness can transform your approach to work. You might recognize when your People-Pleaser is overcommitting you, when your Perfectionist is creating unnecessary stress, or when your Authentic part has important contributions to make to projects.

Parenting and Teaching

Parents and teachers who understand parts often become more compassionate and effective with children. They can recognize when a child's behavior is coming from a protective or hurt part and respond to the underlying needs rather than just the surface behavior.

Community and Social Engagement

Self-led individuals often become positive forces in their communities. When you can stay centered during conflicts, curious about different perspectives, and compassionate toward people who are struggling, you contribute to collective healing.

Spiritual Practice

Many people find that IFS deepens their spiritual life. Understanding parts can help distinguish between spiritual experiences and psychological phenomena. Self-leadership often feels connected to larger spiritual principles of love, wisdom, and service.

The Integration Challenge

One of the ongoing challenges in IFS practice is integration - making sure that your parts work translates into practical life improvements rather than remaining an interesting intellectual framework.

Integration happens through:

Consistent application: Using IFS insights in real-life situations rather than just during internal reflection time.

Behavioral changes: Allowing parts awareness to influence your choices, relationships, and responses to challenges.

Environmental modifications: Changing your life circumstances to better support your parts and Self-leadership.

Relationship shifts: Bringing more authenticity and consciousness to your connections with others.

Values alignment: Making sure your life choices reflect your whole internal system rather than just your most dominant parts.

Maria's Integration Story

Maria had been practicing IFS for three years when she realized her work life was completely out of alignment with her values and authentic interests. Her Achiever and Security parts had driven her to climb the corporate ladder in a field that didn't really interest her, while her Creative and Values-Driven parts felt increasingly frustrated and silenced.

Instead of just understanding this as a parts conflict, Maria decided to take practical action. Over the course of a year, she:

- Negotiated with her Security part about what financial safety really required
- Found ways to express her Creative part through volunteer work and side projects
- Gradually shifted her job responsibilities to include more meaningful projects
- Built up freelance skills that would eventually allow her to leave corporate work
- Created a financial plan that honored both her Security and Values parts

Two years later, Maria was running her own consulting business focused on sustainable business practices. Her Security part felt good about the financial success, her Creative part was engaged by the variety of projects, her Values part was fulfilled by work that made a positive impact, and her Achiever part was satisfied by building something from scratch.

This integration required both internal parts work and external life changes. Maria couldn't have made these changes successfully without understanding her parts, but understanding alone wouldn't have been enough without practical action.

Supporting Others' IFS Journey

One of the natural developments in long-term IFS practice is wanting to share what you've learned with others. This might happen informally with friends and family or more formally through teaching, coaching, or therapeutic work.

When sharing IFS concepts:

Lead by example: The most powerful way to share IFS is by demonstrating Self-leadership in your own life and relationships.

Respect others' readiness: Not everyone is ready for or interested in parts work. Share concepts only when people are genuinely curious.

Avoid diagnosing others: Use IFS to understand your own reactions to others rather than to analyze their internal systems.

Support professional development: If you want to work with others professionally using IFS, get appropriate training and supervision.

Stay humble: Remember that you're always learning and growing in your own IFS practice.

Your Next Steps

As you complete this eight-week introduction to IFS, take some time to reflect on what you've learned and how you want to continue developing your practice:

What parts have you gotten to know better over these eight weeks?

What shifts have you noticed in your relationships, decision-making, or daily experience?

Which IFS concepts and practices feel most valuable for your ongoing development?

What areas of your life would benefit from deeper parts work?

What kind of ongoing practice feels sustainable and interesting to you?

What additional resources or support might help you continue growing?

Resources for Continued Growth

Your IFS journey can be enriched through various resources:

Books: There are many excellent books on IFS and related topics that can deepen your understanding.

Training programs: IFS Institute and other organizations offer workshops and training programs for people interested in deeper learning.

Therapy: Working with an IFS-trained therapist can help you address more complex parts relationships and heal deeper wounds.

Online communities: There are online groups and forums where people share their IFS experiences and support each other's growth.

Retreat programs: Some organizations offer IFS retreats that provide intensive opportunities for internal work.

The Ripple Effects

As you continue developing your IFS practice, you'll likely notice ripple effects that extend far beyond your personal growth:

Your relationships become more authentic as you learn to show up from Self-leadership rather than from reactive parts.

Your work becomes more aligned with your whole self rather than just your achievement or security-oriented parts.

Your parenting or teaching becomes more compassionate as you understand the parts dynamics in children and respond to underlying needs.

Your community involvement becomes more effective as you can stay centered during conflicts and support others' Self-leadership.

Your creative expression becomes more genuine as parts that carry your authentic voice feel safer to emerge.

This is the ultimate promise of IFS work - not just personal healing, but contribution to collective healing. When you learn to coordinate your own internal system with wisdom and compassion, you become a force for wisdom and compassion in the world.

Living from Wholeness

The goal of IFS isn't to eliminate your parts or transcend your humanity. It's to learn to live from the fullness of who you are - all your parts working together under the loving leadership of your Self.

This means honoring your Security part's need for stability while also letting your Adventure part explore new possibilities. It means appreciating your Responsible part's commitment to obligations while also creating space for your Playful part to emerge. It means working with your Perfectionist's high standards while also embracing your Experimental part's willingness to make mistakes.

Living from wholeness means you don't have to choose between being practical and being creative, between being responsible and being spontaneous, between being independent and being connected. You can be all of these things because all of these parts are genuinely part of you.

Your Ongoing Journey

The Internal Family Systems model offers a framework for understanding yourself, but your actual internal family is unique to you. Only you can discover all the parts that make up your system, understand their particular histories and needs, and learn how to coordinate them skillfully.

This is both the challenge and the gift of IFS work - it's ultimately a journey of self-discovery that no one else can take for you. But you don't have to take it alone. Your parts are with you, ready to share their wisdom and contribute their gifts. Your Self is with you, naturally equipped with the curiosity, compassion, and courage needed to lead this internal family.

The world needs people who can think clearly under pressure, respond to conflict with wisdom, and treat both themselves and others with genuine compassion. The world needs people who can access their full range of human capacities and use them skillfully for the benefit of all.

Your IFS practice isn't just personal development - it's preparation for leadership, service, and contribution to the healing our world desperately needs. Every time you respond from Self-leadership rather than from a reactive part, every time you treat your own struggles with curiosity rather than criticism, every time you support someone else in accessing their own wisdom and compassion, you're contributing to collective healing.

Your parts have been waiting your whole life for someone to approach them with the curiosity and compassion you've been developing over these eight weeks. That someone is you. Your Self-leadership has been available all along, ready to coordinate these various aspects of yourself with wisdom and love.

The journey continues. Your internal family is ready to keep growing, learning, and contributing to your life and the lives of everyone you touch. Welcome to the ongoing adventure of living consciously from wholeness.

Your IFS Journey Continues

Congratulations on completing this eight-week introduction to Internal Family Systems. You've covered tremendous ground - from the basic recognition that you have parts through the sophisticated skills of parts dialogue, negotiation, and healing. You've learned to map your internal system, recognize blending states, make decisions that honor your whole self, and maintain Self-leadership in challenging circumstances.

But as this chapter title suggests, this ending is really a beginning. The frameworks and skills you've learned are tools for lifelong growth, healing, and contribution. Your internal family will continue to develop and change as you encounter new life experiences, and your capacity for Self-leadership will deepen as you practice these skills in increasingly complex situations.

The most important thing you've learned is that you are not broken, wrong, or too complicated. You have parts, and that's exactly how humans are designed to be. The goal was never to become a different person - it was to become more fully yourself, with all your parts working together under conscious, compassionate leadership.

Your parts have been faithful companions throughout your life, doing their best to help you survive and thrive with the resources and understanding they had available. Now you have the tools to work with them as conscious allies, honoring their contributions while also providing the coordination they need to serve your whole life effectively.

The world needs people who understand themselves deeply, who can stay centered in chaos, and who can respond to others' struggles with wisdom and compassion. Your ongoing IFS practice prepares you to be this kind of person - not perfect, but conscious; not without challenges, but equipped with skills for working with those challenges creatively and effectively.

Your internal family is ready for whatever comes next. They trust you now in ways they couldn't before, because you've proven that you can listen to them with genuine curiosity and care. They know you won't abandon them or try to eliminate them, but will continue working to understand what they need and help them contribute their gifts to your shared life.

This is just the beginning of a lifelong adventure in conscious, compassionate self-leadership. Your parts are ready. Your Self is equipped. The journey continues.

References

- Anderson, F. G., & Sweezy, M. (2017). *Internal Family Systems Skills Training Manual: Trauma-Informed Treatment for Anxiety, Depression, PTSD & Substance Abuse.* PESI Publishing.
- Clark, G. I., Rock, A. J., Clark, L. H., & Murray-Lyon, K. (2020). Adult attachment, worry and reassurance seeking. *Clinical Psychologist, 24*(3), 294–305.
- Dugas, M. J., & Robichaud, M. (2007). *Cognitive-Behavioral Treatment for Generalized Anxiety Disorder: From Science to Practice.* Routledge.
- Earley, J. (2010). *Self-Therapy for Your Inner Critic: Transforming Self-Criticism into Self-Confidence.* Pattern System Books.
- Evraire, L. E., Fitzpatrick, S., & Hewitt, P. L. (2022). The contribution of attachment styles and reassurance seeking to trust in romantic couples. *Journal of Social and Clinical Psychology, 41*(2), 97–120.
- Earley, J. (2012). *Self-Therapy: A Step-by-Step Guide to Creating Wholeness and Healing Your Inner Child Using IFS.* Pattern System Books.
- Fisher, J. (2017). *Healing the Fragmented Selves of Trauma Survivors: Overcoming Internal Self-Alienation.* Routledge.
- Gottman, J. M. (1999). *The Marriage Clinic: A Scientifically Based Marital Therapy.* W. W. Norton & Company.

- Goulding, R. A., & Schwartz, R. C. (1995). *The Mosaic Mind: Empowering the Tormented Selves of Child Abuse Survivors*. W. W. Norton & Company.

- Hammond, S. A. (2013). *The Thin Book of Appreciative Inquiry* (3rd ed.). Thin Book Publishing.

- Holmes, L. (2007). *The Internal Triangle: New Theories of Female Development*. Jason Aronson.

- Jack, D. C., & Dill, D. (1992). The Silencing the Self Scale: Schemas of intimacy associated with depression in women. *Psychology of Women Quarterly, 16*(1), 97–106.

- Johnson, S. M. (2019). *Attachment Theory in Practice: Emotionally Focused Therapy (EFT) for Individuals, Couples, and Families*. Guilford Press.

- Kabat-Zinn, J. (2013). *Full Catastrophe Living: Using the Wisdom of Your Body and Mind to Face Stress, Pain, and Illness* (Rev. ed.). Bantam Books.

- Neff, K. D. (2015). *Self-Compassion: The Proven Power of Being Kind to Yourself* (Paperback ed.). William Morrow Paperbacks.

- Schwartz, R. C. (2001). *Introduction to the Internal Family Systems Model*. Trailheads Publications.

- Schwartz, R. C., & Sweezy, M. (2019). *Internal Family Systems Therapy* (2nd ed.). Guilford Press.

- Siegel, D. J. (2012). *The Developing Mind: How Relationships and the Brain Interact to Shape Who We Are* (2nd ed.). Guilford Press.

- Siegel, D. J. (2020). *The Developing Mind: How Relationships and the Brain Interact to Shape Who We Are* (3rd ed.). Guilford Press.

- Stone, H., & Stone, S. (1989). *Embracing Our Selves: The Voice Dialogue Manual.* New World Library.

- Tatkin, S. (2012). *Wired for Love: How Understanding Your Partner's Brain and Attachment Style Can Help You Defuse Conflict and Build a Secure Relationship.* New Harbinger Publications.

- van der Kolk, B. A. (2014). *The Body Keeps the Score: Brain, Mind, and Body in the Healing of Trauma.* Penguin Books.

- Webb, J. (2012). *Running on Empty: Overcome Your Childhood Emotional Neglect.* Morgan James Publishing.

- Young, J. E., Klosko, J. S., & Weishaar, M. E. (2003). *Schema Therapy: A Practitioner's Guide.* Guilford Press.

Printed by Libri Plureos GmbH in Hamburg, Germany